JOY

THROUGH THE

JOURNEY

DENNIS A. MCINTYRE
and
KENT CAMMACK

Joy Through the Journey

Published 2025

Printed in the United States of America

First Edition

ISBN (softcover): 978-1-963380-90-3
ISBN (hardcover): 978-1-967842-00-1
ISBN (e-book): 978-1-963380-91-0

For information, address:

Holzer Books LLC
8 The Green, Ste. A
Dover, Delaware 19901 USA

For information about special discounts available for bulk purchases, sales promotions, and educational needs, contact:

info@holzerbooksllc.com
+1 (888) 901-7776

holzerbooksLLC©

Contents

Acknowledgements

Sandye and I would like to thank Ginger Cook for help in editing this book, and Rob Briscoe for his support and always believing in God's plan for our story. In addition, there is no way we could list all of the people that have been friends, work acquaintances, church friends, or who helped us over the years. Please accept our deepest thanks for being a part of lives during this journey, you know who you are.

Please visit our website: www.GodRestoringSandy.wordpress.com, or the QR Code to get more information on the book, our giving ministry, pictures, or dramatic videos.

Preface

The road of Life is unique for every individual. Millions of decisions are made through each change in direction or event. Retracing our steps would be an impossible task. At best, we might recall the major events that made a difference in our lives or the lives of others. Travelling back to those places where our journey began may provide some answers to one question, "Has my life made a difference?"

As we near the end of our time on earth, another question may enter our minds. "Is this the end or is there more?" As a Christian, my hope is on eternity and a glorious reunion with friends and family. "Who will be there to greet me in heaven?" Reflecting on that question takes me on one more journey. Perhaps, the trip will provide some answers.

Kent and Sandye Christmas 2024 at the Bible museum

Foreword by Dr. William H. Stuart

Dr. William H. Stuart is one of the most renowned M.S. Neurologists. He is recently retired in 2024 after focusing on Multiple Sclerosis patients in his 64 year career. Over the last 65 years there is a good chance that know one has seen more MS patients that Dr. Stuart in the world. We are proud to bring to you this foreword is from Dr. Stuart.

"Sandra Pietropoli (Sandye and her husband Kent) were patients of mine from 1995-2003 then 2005-2019 totaling 22 years. Sandra was diagnosed with Progressive M.S. in 1991 which is a form of the disease that presents a slow deteriorating mental and physical state over the years. Everyone who has this disease is affected differently. No two patients are the same. Unfortunately, in Sandra's case, the medicine available in the 1990's was not advanced enough to stop the progression of Sandra's symptoms causing a severe mental and physical disability. There were various medications for treatments of M.S. prescribed throughout the 1980's, 90's, and early 2000's. With no cure for M.S. these drugs were designed at the time to assist in halting or slowing down the progression of the disease. Recent medical developments in the last few years have now made it possible for some patients to experience a reversal or stop the symptoms of M.S. The M.S. medical field is now making great strides towards a cure.

The sudden reversal that Sandra experienced in 2016 to my knowledge is unheard of; if not extremely rare. Short of performing a brain biopsy (which is not possible while she is alive), what happened to Sandra cannot be medically explained.

The book "Joy Through the Journey" depicts a great true story (to my knowledge) of Sandra and her husband Kent. The percentage of men that choose to remain and care for their wives year after year is a heartbreaking low number. This couple's positive remarkable story of thriving and giving to others against all odds is an example for all of us to read and thoroughly enjoy and emulate. I highly recommend that everyone read this book. It has been a pleasure working with this couple for 22 years."

Dr. William H. Stuart

1984-85 – Founding member of the American Society of Neuroimaging.

1988 – Focused specifically on Multiple Sclerosis (MS)

1991 – Developed the Multiple Sclerosis Comprehensive Care and Research Center at the Shepherd Center in Atlanta, GA.

2001 – Founded the MS Center of Atlanta (now going by the name of the Atlanta Neuroscience Institute), which is one of the largest and most comprehensive M.S. Care programs in the U.S.

Foreword by Lawrence Warder

My late wife introduced me to Kent and Sandye in 1990 at an event sponsored by restaurants on Hilton Head. Kent was in a bartender's race which he lost. We became friends. Kent and I talked often about his future. He said that he wanted to get his college degree, but I didn't think that he was mature enough. I was wrong!

Kent graduated and married Sandye after she was diagnosed with MS. Most men would have run from that responsibility, but not Kent. He went on to a challenging career.

What I admired was their commitment to leading a fulfilling life. They travelled often and visited us in London in the late 1990's while Sandye was wheelchair bound and went on to visit other European countries. They didn't let life's difficulties stop them while Sandye could still travel. They visited us in Dallas and Hilton Head and Sandye fulfilled a dream of hers; she parachuted from a plane.

They persevered through many ups and downs. In addition to dealing with their issues they also focused on helping others through their non-profit organization.

I have tremendous respect for them both.

Lawrence Warder

Global Director of Operations, Deloitte Consulting (retired)

Chief Financial Officer, US Dept of Education (retired)

Introduction

It's hard to believe where the road called "Life" has led me. I can only imagine a far different destination, without joy, love, or peace. I would have pictured my life being drunk on the beach or broke in Las Vegas, but God had far better plans. He weaved two unique souls together in a bond of love and unending joy that would confound the Hollywood script writers. Although our journey is ongoing, we feel compelled to share where we have been with the hope that others enjoy the ride and are blessed beyond measure.

Some things are unexplainable. When I see a caterpillar form a cocoon and then emerge as a beautiful butterfly, I still am amazed. Diamonds are formed by pressurized coal. How can something so mundane turn into such brilliance? I am further amazed that people justify these things as the result of chance and not design. Looking back at where life began for me and where I am today is equally inexplicable, except for the fact that I know without any doubt that everything was designed. Growing up without a father's wisdom shaped my early life with poor decisions, but my heavenly father saw a chunk of marble to be chiseled into his masterpiece. Slowly and methodically, He began to cut away, introducing people and opportunities as tools in the process. If you enjoy love stories, this is for you. If you need to laugh, please read on. If you think that life has dealt you a poor hand, I encourage you to share this wonderful ride with me. If you feel that your life is without meaning, let me assure you that is not true. Some of the most difficult trials in your life can end up being the most rewarding. The pleasure that I found in a bottle or at a blackjack table is nothing compared to the joy I feel today and look forward to even greater joy in the future. Just when you thought you had seen it all God overwhelms all of us with a miracle that the medical world was forced to confront. There is no doubt Jesus took control for all of us to see.

Hilton Head or Bust

As I stood looking down over Sandye in the hospital bed, I was blown away at the calmness in her face. She was asleep and looked at peace. No one would know by looking at her that she fell into some kind of coma. It was 11:30 on Saturday 10/01/2016, and she had been incoherent for an hour. Dr. Bielo, the doctor assigned to us at Piedmont Hospital in Atlanta, was out in the hallway at the station waiting as if she knew something was going to happen to Sandye soon. Carly, who just became a nurse three months prior, was checking in on occasion. Sandye had just come back into the room from getting a brain scan. Now there was no one else in the room accept her, me and my prayers. Fearing that I was probably going to lose her, my heart was racing. It was all I could do to not scream at the top of my lungs. In a desperate plea I started singing some of the Christian songs that we had listened to together. "Jesus, Jesus, precious Jesus" and "It is well with my soul" head the list.

> Kent: "Sandye, we have so much to do. We have been through so much over almost 30 years together. I believe God has many more plans for us going forward. If it is your will Lord, please bring her back. Sandye, I love you so much."

It was like all thirty years were racing through my brain. My mind flashed back to 1987 when we first met. I was twenty-four years old and had no clue about life or the Lord. Work hard and play hard has always been the themes of my family. My grandmother set the mark by being married five times during the 1900's. Perhaps it was gambling or drinking that formed my compulsive all-in competitive drive. It could have been the lack of a father figure in my life that created my cry for attention personality. My reckless abandon and carefree attitude of living on the edge drew my friends towards me. I craved the attention and wasn't afraid to say what everybody was thinking. Mom had already divorced four husbands and was dating someone new. I needed a change. This is my journey. My name is Kent.

My mother broke the mold of every stereotype. She was five-foot-ten, very beautiful and a magnet for men. At eighteen, she won third place behind two petite blonde girls in a city-wide beauty contest, which tall girls were not winning at that time. She burned bras, wore fancy hats, and was divorced before it was mainstream. Without family guidelines, she was in a survival mode and was not going to lose. The accepted choice for women at the time was to become a housewife. She chose to be a schoolteacher on a fixed income. She was exceptional at maximizing opportunities, which her children would experience. We were always included in her school parties, often held at our home. The most notable were pool parties with two or three other families. We swam all day while the adults played games and drank hard.

In the seventies, while married to her second husband, the hard work and partying increased. I was on the swim team, played various team sports including, football, baseball, basketball, and bowling. Every weekend in the winter we would catch the train in downtown Denver to Winter Park to ski. It was a two hour ride up and two hours back through the Moffit Tunnel. Due to all the tile in the tunnel we used to call it "the largest bathroom in the world." We would ski every Saturday, and I would pay for my expenses by selling candy and sodas on the train. The return trip back to Denver is where I learned, at ten years old, how to be a salesman. I had a cooler filled with colas and candy bars. The passengers were very tired from the day of skiing, dehydrated and hungry. I knew this would be lucrative just walking down the aisle with cokes, candy and a smile.

Passenger: "How Much is it for a coke?"

Kent: "A dollar."

Passenger: "Are you kidding. That is way overpriced."

Kent: (mumbling) "Oh, never mind." (started walking away)

Passenger: "Hey kid. Come back here. Here's your dollar you little conman."

I did very well selling candy and sodas on that train ride. Luckily, I didn't get shoved into the small bathroom or get thrown off the train. I learned how to make my own money. After mom's second divorce we were on our own. I gravitated towards coaches and schoolteachers as my father figure. One coach helped get me hooked on gambling. I loved the distraction and the rush of winning.

I loved my mother more than anyone on the planet. I was fourteen when we moved to Las Vegas. Mom worked at a casino. She wore one of those lacey low-cut cocktail dresses. When I saw those skirts, I would say, "here come the booby girls." Mom made good money. She also introduced me to the gambling bug. Me, my brother and little sister would play games at Circus Circus and won a lot of stuffed animals, most of the time while mom was working. Then, at the end of the summer, one of her boyfriends from Denver decided to fly into Las Vegas, convince mom to marry him, move back to Denver, and make a family together. He was six-foot-eight and mom was five-ten. They dominated any room that they entered.

He lived on extreme highs and lows. Drugs, drinking, hard work, and heavy gambling made for a normal week. He owned a successful pallet company and mom decided to go into the real estate business. Monday night football steak night was great when he won. When his team lost, all the kids scattered and hightailed it out of the house to flee from that angry, Goliath of a man. Mom loved the high emotional times when it was good but, look out, when the lows hit. There were times when she had to apply heavy make-up to hide her black eyes. Somehow mom looked back and saw those times as being the best. I never saw things that way. He did teach me a lot about gambling. I thought that I was good at it but was horrible and never knew when to stop.

I was fun-loving and dying for attention. I was a child actor, playing "Christopher Robin" in Winnie the Pooh. I was even paid thirty-five dollars a week to be in dinner theater musicals. I was a horrible singer, but they wanted me for my acting skills. They told me to mouth the words when singing in *The Sound of Music* production and was actually referenced in the Denver Post Newspaper. My ego was so big that my sister kicked me out of the car while I was showing off the new TV that I purchased. I walked a mile home carrying the box holding the TV. My personality and hard work helped me get a fully paid scholarship to Colorado University, in Boulder, Colorado. Personal issues, no self-control, and bad relationships haunted me. I ended up dropping out of college after four years without completing a degree. I then started waiting tables in the morning shift at the Double Tree Hotel restaurant.

My Honda 750 motorcycle had been taking me to work at 5:30 AM at the Double Tree Hotel restaurant earning thirty-five dollars a day. A couple I knew invited me to Hilton Head, South Carolina for a week-long vacation. At twenty-four years old my testosterone was flying. The thought of making the move involved very little soul searching. On one side of the scale, I was making thirty-five dollars a day going into work at five o'clock in the morning. Colorado has a beautiful mountain view, but below zero winters. On the other hand, in Hilton Head. I could earn one-hundred dollars a day, with bikinis that would fit inside a shot glass, and bars that stayed open until six A.M. You make the call.

When my mother learned about my decision to leave, she was despondent. Currently single, as dysfunctional as she was, she always encouraged me to experience things for myself. The problem was that I only had a motorcycle for transportation and about a thousand dollars to my name. Since the bike could not haul my belongings, it had to be sold and another vehicle take its place. My mother's latest boyfriend worked in a construction business and offered to sell me an old, paneled van for seven hundred dollars. The price was right, but to say that the van needed some work was a big understatement. The hood was being held down by a bent coat hanger, which stretched across the smashed front end. The shag carpet on the ceiling inside made a strong statement. When I turned on the dome light, everything turned pink. I called it my pink love light. Then there was a bumper sticker on the dash which read, "ASS, GAS, or GRASS, nobody rides for FREE"." I thought that I was so cool! Every fill up would also need a quart or two of oil added. Needless to say, it offered the needed transportation and storage room for everything that I owned in the world, so off I went. I had recurring thoughts of Jim Carey in the movie "Dumb and Dumber." I remember yelling, "Yes. This is going to be GREAT!"

The trip east would take me through hundreds of miles of flat land in

Kansas, where civilization might be seen far in the distance. Driving over sixty miles per hour would turn the van into a rattletrap. Since, I did not have a timeframe in mind, the slower speeds did not pose a problem. I placed a large glass deep-rock water bottle in the back that was half filled with coins. I planned to use the money for gas. The trip began as my two-thousand-mile adventure.

At one point right before I was ready to move, I was driving the van and had to hit the brakes hard. The bottle of coins surged forward and I heard SMASH! Before I could stop it, glass shattered and coins flew everywhere. I pulled over and collected as many coins as I could find and placed them into a laundry bag. Later, I took the bag into a bank to exchange them for cold hard cash. The teller helped count the money and started crying out.

Teller: "Ooh, ouch. What else is in here?"

Kent: "I'm so sorry. I had the coins in a large glass jar and it broke."

Teller: "You may be nice but I don't usually have cuts and dirt all over me when counting coins."

I apologized profusely, I shoved $189.15 into my pocket and started my big venture.

After driving out of Colorado I was eleven miles outside Hays, Kansas, side by side with a large eighteen-wheel truck. Then the hanger holding the hood down let go. The hood flew up and smashed the windshield to smithereens. Screaming at the top of my lungs while swerving and trying not to get run over by the truck, I was able to pull to the side of the road. The window was still held together but looked like a jigsaw puzzle.

Somehow, I could still see through it. Now, my goal was to get to Hays and replace the window. Running the engine up to about forty-five miles an hour caused the fragments of glass to dislodge from the window. They started flying and hitting me, making cuts all over my face.

"Oooh, ouch, ooh..." I had to pull over again. I looked into a mirror to see the damage to my face. It was not a pleasant sight. I had to do something. I looked into the back of the van at everything I owned. Thinking I was smart, I found the ironing board that I had loaded and began smashing the windshield from the inside out of the van. I did not want to litter and leave the glass on the road. It came out in one big piece of what was left, and I put that piece in the back of the van. I started driving again and now I was ten miles from Hays, Kansas but tried to limit my speed to fifty.

Well, if you know Kansas in the summer, there is nothing but crops as far as you can see. Where there are crops there are millions of bugs. Large bugs began to hit my face and choking me. Now there were juicy bug splats on the fresh cuts on my face. It wasn't pretty! Once again, I pulled over, now only nine miles from Hays. One thing my mom had taught was there are five different ways to figure out any challenge. I sat there looking at everything that I owned for a solution. I did not have my motorcycle anymore, but I did have my MOTORCYCLE HELMET! Yes! Then I continued down the road with a new sense of achievement. With my helmet on, I sucked a soda through a straw and was happy as a clam. Cars would drive by and honk. The kids inside would point at me and I would wave through the opening in the window out the front of the van. I felt like John Candy just took over my body in the movie "Planes Trains and Automobiles." This trip had all the makings of a best comedy movie. I was now going to make it to Hays, Kansas!

I stopped at a gas station in Hays to check on a windshield replacement. They were able to replace it with most of the money that I had with me.

I called my sister in Oklahoma City for financial help. She told me to just get to her house and she would help me get the rest of the way. After a well needed rest in Oklahoma, I was making great time, traveling through state after state. I was about a hundred miles from Little Rock Arkansas, and I knew that I should have checked the oil at the last rest stop (I had two fresh quarts). The engine began to cough and sputter and then BOOM. It blew up belching black smoke everywhere. I limped to a stop along the road.

I sat there for a couple hours. There were no cell phones back then. A police car spotted me and stopped.

Officer: "How can I help you, sir?"

Kent: "My engine is blown."

Officer: "There's a garage a few miles back. I can call a tow for you."

Kent: "That would be great. Thank you."

The van was towed to the filling station, where two large local mechanics met me. One of them removed the coat hanger and opened the hood. The other reached for the long dip stick and pulled it out. At the very end was a big clump of melted engine. The mechanics eyes were wide open.

Mechanic 1: "You're gonna be here a while!" (In a long southern draw)

Kent: "Oh NO."

Mechanic 1: "You need a new engine."

Mechanic 2: "I never changed a whole engine before, papa. Kin I do it?"

Kent: "How much will that cost?"

Mechanic 1: "About $700."

Kent: "OH NO! I don't have that kind of money. I'm on my way to a new job."

Mechanic 2: (with a very strong southern accent) Wail, you kin take the Continental Trailways Bus across the street. It will take you anywhere in the world."

Kent: "Oh NO! How long will changing the engine take?"

Mechanic 1: "couple of days, need to go to Sevier County for a used engine."

Mechanic 1: "There's good eatin at the café and soft beds at the motel!"

Kent: "I need to make a call, and I will let you know."

The two mechanics discussed the situation, while I made my way to a diner next to the station. The men looked like mountain men in dirty bib overalls but seemed to enjoy the challenge before them. This was not a comfortable feeling; I did not have enough to pay for the new engine. The men and area made me think I was in the movie "Deliverance." I kept hearing the theme song on the banjo in my head "da ding ding, ding ding, ding ding ding." Oh boy that was creepy. I discussed my situation with an old girl friend, who agreed to transfer the funds. Since the work would take time, I also needed money to stay at the motel nearby. I told the workers to go ahead with the work and then got me a room. Except for a brief trip to the café for food, I isolated myself in the room and would jog up and down the road at daylight always watching my back. I was not a hockey fan but watched it on ESPN the whole long week.

The work was completed a seven scary days later, and the bill came to thirteen-hundred dollars. EEE gads!

Kent: "I thought you said it was for $700."

Mechanic 1: "YUP it was a bit higher than that, heh heh."

Kent: "I need to call someone to get the money transferred to your account."

Mechanic 1: "What's this transfer business. I never heard of that. We like to work with cash?"

Kent: "It's a way for money to be sent from a bank to your account."

I called my friend once more to ask for more money.

Kent: "I am so sorry. This has been an experience. I hate to bother you again. Can you help me with the motel cost? I never wanted to put you in this situation."

It was too bad the only person that I felt was a girl friend from the past.

Friend: "That's okay, Kent. I will transfer the money. Good luck to you."

Kent: "Thank you so much. Words cannot express it."

I do not know what I would have done without the kindness of this Lady. I have lost track of her over these years but would love to pay her back if I could find her. I gave her the station's bank information and she made the transfer. Minutes later, I returned to inform the station manager that the money has been transferred. He yelled at the two mechanics, "I'm gonna check this out. Hold him there until I return."

The mechanics stood tall with their arms folded like bodyguards. It was not a pleasant moment. Then the owner returned shouting, "I don't know how he did it but the money's there. Let him go." I sighed a huge breath of relief while I felt like I was in a scene for the Andy Griffith show.

I paid the motel bill and resumed my journey to paradise. My two-day trip was now stretched to over a week and a half. The hope was that there would be no more disruptions. Upon entering Memphis, the water pump blew at 11:00 at night. I said, "forget this." I listened to the water hose screeching and went to sleep for the night, so both the van and I could cool off. It turned out to be an easy fix. Two weeks after leaving Denver, I arrived in Hilton Head by the amazing Atlantic Ocean. I had finally made it to my dream destination in my "Chick Magnet Custom Van."

***

Chip, chip, chip. The master sculpturer slowly hammered away at the marble slab. A trip, that should have taken three or four days, was filled with trials and setbacks. With each one I was learning patience that was in direct opposition to my fast paced out of control lifestyle. The sculpturer knew that the final masterpiece needed many alterations.

Love is in the Air

By the age of twenty-four most people might say that they had a plan forward. My fun-loving riotous living and lack of a college degree had not prepared me for what was about to happen next. A friend and his wife opened their home to me in Hilton Head, South Carolina, when I arrived. It was May of 1987 when I rolled onto that island, which at one time was barely inhabited and once had wild boar with no bridge to access it. Now it was starting to grow into a premier vacation destination. The only plan that I had was to find work, save money until I could afford a place of my own, and have as much fun as I could possibly have. I was able to work at two or three different restaurants using my serving skills, while still looking for the best paying job. The paneled "piece of work" van was hanging in there to get me around this twelve-mile island that was shaped like a Nike tennis shoe.

In August I accepted a waiter position at the William F. Pelican Restaurant near the entrance of the island. This was a seafood restaurant that filled up fast, with a beautiful view out over the marsh with stunning sunsets. It was a three-story building with the bar in the basement. A large flight of stairs led up to a platform where you entered the kitchen. Be prepared to get out of the way of someone barreling through with a full tray of food headed up another huge flight of stairs to the dining room. This job was like a track meet running up and down stairs sweating like a pig and trying not to get run over. There were times when I would get to the table and sweat would drop off my forehead onto the plate of food for the awaiting customer. They weren't happy but what could I do. The money was good though. By the time we were done with the shift we smelled like a sweaty fish. Our nickname for the Restaurant was the "Smelly Pelly". Needless to say, it should not have been a Restaurant and has since been converted to the Island's Welcome Center.

One day while shining silverware before a shift in the dining room, I looked over and saw a server, bending down to get some condiments from the bottom shelf. He was a male server who was known as a prankster. While he bent way over in a vulnerable position, this pretty blonde waitress walked by him and knocked him over onto the floor. She could not resist the opportunity to pull a prank on the prankster. He caught himself from falling down the flight of stairs, while she kept going, laughing at the top of her lungs. She walked over to another blonde and said, "Brenda, I finally got Kevin." They high fived and laughed as Kevin grinned thinking about how to get her back. The scene was like something out of an old slapstick comedy like "I Love Lucy" or "The Three Stooges." The ladies were free spirited and enjoyed a fun time. I knew for sure that I had to get to know these women. They were close to my age, both blonde and beautiful. Their names are Sandye and Brenda. I ran over to Sandye to officially meet her.

Kent: "Hey, you two are funny."

Sandye: "We get by. When did you start here Kent?"

Kent: "August 15th"

Brenda: "We're new here too."

Kent: "You both seem to have the best time in this job."

Sandye: "You can't dwell on the negatives. Besides, he had it coming." (said with a big smile)

Kent: "I love to have fun. Would you like to join me for a drink when we wind down after the shift."

Sandye: "I'm not sure if three is a crowd; let me talk to Brenda and we will let you know."

Later that night, as the shift was winding down, Sandye came up to me and said:

Sandye: "Brenda and I agreed that you can go out with us on one condition."

Kent: "Oh yeah, what's that?"

Sandye: "That you pay for the night." (with another smile on her face)

I was up for the challenge and agreed. What I didn't know at the time was that I would be paying for those two ladies for a long, long time.

They agreed to meet me at a local bar. We had to go home and peel off the soaked smelly uniforms, shower, and change into casual clothes. I had on shorts and a t-shirt. They came in all dressed up. My heart seemed to skip a beat. What a transformation from their uniforms. They were both absolutely beautiful. The style at the time was the bigger the hair the better the look. I referred to them as the blonde bombshells. Sandye was blonde bombshell number one and Brenda was number two. Later, I called them "BB1" and "BB2."

During the evening, two men began hassling the bartender. Sandye stepped in and got in their faces.

> Sandye: "Oh NO. You don't talk to my friend that way, she is doing the best job she can."

The men were obnoxious, but Sandye held her ground.

> Sandye: "No one treats a woman like that." (which amazed me)

The men were a bit shocked that a woman would stand them down. They backed off and decided to mind their own business. I was impressed. Sandye had shown a side of her that was attractive beyond her outer looks. She stood up for people in a way that I could never dream of. She was a full-blooded Italian girl with a huge heart. The girls offered to chip in when paying the bill, but I was proud to uphold my end of the deal and pay it.

I might have been wild on the outside, but I was a bit shaky on the inside when it came to getting close to women. I finally worked up the nerve to ask Sandye out on a date without Brenda being present. We decided to meet on our day off at the Ruby Tuesday Restaurant on the island.

I needed to polish up on my "one-liners," since no one ever taught me what I should say or what was appropriate when engaging women. Up until then I would say whatever came to my mind. Sandye was beautiful with long curly voluptuous hair. As I sat across from her, I always wondered about women's hair in general. We ordered food, and without a second thought I initiated the following conversation:

Kent: "So Sandye, is that your real hair color?"

Absolutely flabbergasted, she had the following reply:

Sandye: "Excuse me, what did you just say?"

Then there was a long awkward silence.

Kent: "I meant no harm. I was just wondering. I really am sorry if I was out of line."

Sandye: "I should get up and leave right now, but we will see this out. YOU need to know that women never forget when men say stupid things."

You know what, they don't forget! We ended up having a couple drinks and enjoyed laughing spontaneously together. As we were exiting the restaurant we were walking towards my van.

Sandye: "Whoa, look at that PIECE OF SHIT!"

Kent: "UH! That is mine."

Sandye: "You have got to be kidding me! Does it start-up?"

She vowed never to ride in that van, Her Oldsmobile Firenza became a better choice for transportation when we went out. I guess my van was only for select people to ride in. One day Sandye and I were riding in her car when I said something obnoxious. I don't remember what it was, but I do remember what she said.

> Sandye: "I don't know who you are referring to, but there are only two people in this car, and I know you are not talking to me."

Those words echoed in my head. My old self was about to get a strong lesson on how to treat people. Disrespect was not in her vocabulary. Although I might not have intended it that way, I knew that I had to be more thoughtful before speaking to her or any ladies for that matter. I learned that if ladies can help guide men early in a relationship and not settle or compromise for unethical or immoral words, then we can become the gentlemen we are supposed to be.

Sandye and I began meeting after our shifts for a nightcap and started sharing. We had a lot in common as we both enjoyed nice impulsive spur of the moment dinners, time on the beach and travelling. During one of our conversations, Sandye shared that her life needed a change in direction and picked Hilton Head totally randomly on a map. She had three Islands to choose from and just pointed at Hilton Head and moved there "sight unseen." Wow! We figured out later that we both moved to Hilton Head in May the same week, possibly even the same day. She moved from Charleston, West Virginia and I was on a collision course with her fresh out of Denver Colorado.

She was living in a condo on the beach down on the far end of the Island. The four-hundred dollar a month rent was high, but a chef friend split it with her and slept on the couch. It seemed a bit awkward. He had to walk through her bedroom to get to the bathroom. She liked him (he looked like Jerry Garcia from the Grateful Dead) but they were just friends. One night we were drinking and Sandye offered for me to stay over and not drive all the way to the other end of the island to my apartment. I slept with her in her bedroom, but no "funny business." I scooted out to work early the next day.Chef Jack left $200 on her nightstand which was his monthly rent. When Sandye saw this money, she thought it was from me. She told Brenda that I left her $200, and she didn't even have to sleep with me. At this rate she was going to be rich! They both laughed.

The beach became one of our favorite spots. I would run on the sand in the morning before my shift. The sand on Hilton Head is hard packed. Sandye and I would ride "fat wheel tire" bikes all over the island while keeping a constant eye out for dolphins. It was absolutely beautiful. We spent endless hours together laughing, eating, and dancing at the Holiday Inn on the beach. Sunrises and sunsets were spectacular. After months of close intimate times, while we were looking out at one of the sunsets, we started sharing some of our most private details. Sandye shared that she needed a new start because she had a very difficult divorce from the first love of her life. I could tell this hurt her very deeply. Her compassion allowed me to share that my previous personal relationships could be counted on one hand. I also felt the need to finally bare my soul and share, that while I had no father to speak of, I was crying out for affection of a father figure. A coach and another teacher sexually abused me when I was eight to thirteen years of age. It was painful to discuss. These experiences messed me up in the head and made close relationships uncomfortable. Up until that point, I made self centered bad decisions with personal relationships, work, and school. We were both looking for new lives, which drove us to Hilton Head. We were great friends first and foremost. The physical love came later and was very special.

***

Chip, chip, chip. The master sculpturer needed to get rid of more imper-fections. Sandye demonstrated respect for people and a willingness to take a stand when necessary. I learned a valuable lesson about showing respect. My past kept me in bondage but I needed resolution. Sandye may be just the one to provide the help that I was needing.

Best Friends

U p until this point we had separate living arrangements. We needed to be together in a larger place. All three of us rented a home about a block from the beach. Chef Jack stayed in the upstairs loft and made great New England Clam chowder. It was a great situation for now. My mother was working on her fourth marriage, and Sandye wasn't planning on getting married ever again. We were child free. We were very close and I was falling head over heels for her. Since we both enjoyed taking trips, we decided to pool our resources. I was constantly working and making good money. We would take ten dollars or more from each shift's tips and put them in a box. Whenever we reached fifteen-hundred dollars, we would go on a cruise in the Caribbean or fly to the Bahamas. Our first trip was to the Bahamas. We stayed at a pink hotel for her birthday. She planned everything. We wanted to go where the locals went to hang out and explore. We asked a couple of guys where to go for local food and fun. They started taking us down a back road. I was oblivious to the situation, but Sandye stopped in her tracks and said:

Sandye: "Let's go back right now!"

Kent: "What and miss the fun."

Sandye: "Listen to me. I am serious we must leave right now."

I trusted her judgement, and as we hurried back the way we came, while the guys were hollering for us to return. When we reached a familiar place Sandye said:

Sandye: "That was not a gut feeling. Something very strong came upon me that we were in serious danger."

I never found out what was going to happen, but there was no doubt that she was right with her feeling. Something guided her to protect us. The next day we decided to stay in plain view of other tourists and went to the Atlantis Hotel. There we shared a two-hundred-dollar dinner and enjoyed the beautiful stars while eating Lobster Thermador. It started an incredible passionate joy of food and travel that would help us through all the incredible challenges that were to come. We gambled that night, which fueled the strong compulsive nature ingrained in me to work hard and play hard.

Because we lived close to the beach, it afforded the opportunity for me to run a lot. Even though I was on my feet most of the day at the restaurant, running was a great stress reliever. I started entering local races on the island and worked my way up to running my first 10 K (6.2 miles). The race was held in Beaufort, S.C. about forty-five minutes away. Sandye was very supportive of my running and came to watch me. The race wound over two long bridges, and as I passed the two-thirds point, it started to pour down rain. At first it felt refreshing and cooled my body, but then my sneakers started to get very heavy and wet. It felt like I was running in cement shoes. This was my first 10K race. I was bound and determined to finish. As I came around the last turn the rain really came down. I knew I was close, so I was running as hard as I could. The spectators left due to the weather. With my last breath before the finish line, I glanced left and only one person remained, barely able to hold her umbrella. Over the rain I heard:

Sandye: "Go Kent, Go Kent!"

I couldn't believe my eyes and ears. It fueled me to finish strong. As soon as I finished, I turned back to find Sandye alone, soaking wet. She had a cute smile on her face and said:

Sandye: "Good Job."

Kent: "Why didn't you stay in the car like everyone else?"

She threw her arms around me and said, "I'm here for you."

After one fun day at the beach during a romantic evening, I couldn't stand it anymore. I was about to bust and said, "I love You." Sandye responded without hesitation, "I love you too." This was only the second person I ever said this to. I knew everything would be better and different going forward.

By then I started to work at the Crazy Crab Restaurant in the famous Harbour Town Yacht Club by the lighthouse. Sandye also worked at a local dinner theater. Brenda and a girl from England named Avril, who Sandye met at the other restaurant, became Sandye's best friends. Avril was married to a man named Jose, who was from Majorca Spain. In the future Avril and Jose would have to go back to Spain. Sandye and Avril dreamed of a time when we could go and visit them there. Brenda became a constant companion. Her training as a marine offered a contrast in their personalities but they were inseparable. The "Blonde Bombshells" had a lot in common." They were both strong-willed, determined, loved shopping for good deals, traveling, and they were both "Foodies." They would ride those fun beach bikes all over, finding short cuts to the nice hotels for lunch, shopping and drinks. They loved spending time dressing up while enjoying a cocktail or two. Getting all dolled up with make-up and "dressing up to the nines" (which meant to me, ooh la la) was special to them. One morning, Sandye was looking at the local paper called "The Island Packet."

> Sandye: "Hey! The Hotel Intercontinental is having a black-tie dinner event with a fashion show featuring designer furs. I got to call Brenda, and you must rent a tuxedo, because we are going to the Ball."

I was always up for a good time, so we set it up. The girls wore stunning full-length dresses with jewelry (costume, but you would never know it) and I think this was the first time I had ever worn a tuxedo. With a lady on each arm, we were styling at this soiree! The models floated down the runway with top-of-the-line fur coats, fur head wraps and hats. Anything that was fur and fancy was flaunted all over the ballroom. We knew that we craved to have more special occasions like this for a long time to come. As the show and food were winding down, the announcer invited the guests to come backstage and peruse the furs. I realized that this event was also an opportunity for the show to sell the merchandise.

> Sandye: "Well my friends, (with a big smile on her face) when

in Rome lets go backstage and partake in the festivities!"

There we tried on every kind of fur you could think of and snapped glamour photo shots for memories sake. Sandye, covered in this gorgeous full-length fur, leaned her head to the left rubbing the huge soft fur on her face. She was in her glory.

Sandye; "My mom never got the chance to do this. She raised four kids and never got this chance. She always used to dress up at home for dinner with her family, dreaming of these kinds of moments. This is for you mom!"

At this time Brenda was wearing a fur that looked like some type of Russian hat with a matching fur coat. She looked mysterious and beautiful like something out of a James Bond film.

Kent and Sandye (Bond and Natasha)

Sandye: "We need a man to chauffer us. Hey Kent, put on that men's fur coat."

The ladies must have put a trance on me. The next thing I knew, we were posing for glamour shots dreaming of being anywhere in the world. The girls were on cloud nine and so was I, because I was with them. We loved having fun and dreaming of the next venture. As I was coming out of the rest room walking down the hallway at the Hotel Intercontinental, I looked out the window and could not believe my eyes. Sandye grabbed one of those luggage handler carts and told Brenda to get on for the ride. I ran out the door.

Kent: "Hey what are you ladies doing?"

Sandye: "Hold on Brenda we are going for a ride!"

Brenda stood on the part where we would usually put our luggage and Sandye started pushing her down this slow decline. As they picked up speed Brenda screamed.

Brenda: "WHEEEEEE!"

Wearing high heels, Sandye was pushing while running down the lobby entrance laughing and howling with fun. There was nobody around to stop them. To them it was pure joy. This would set the stage for a lifetime of friendship with huge moments, classic birthdays, weddings, trips and ultimate joy through the Journey with the "Blonde Bombshells" and me.

That winter Sandye, Brenda and I decided to go to Key Largo to work and earn money during the Winter. Chef Jack recommended this place called Ocean Reef. It was a high-end resort, where the vacationers had no worries, all expenses were charged, and they did not take cash. We got a job working a breakfast and lunch area outside in the heat where the diners would enjoy a dolphin show. Brenda picked up a night server position where she was partnered with this fun, free spirited guy name Robert. She was having a great time, but Sandye and I did not. The customers were treated like Kings and Queens. When we walked behind this large row of trees blocking our cinder block apartments, it was a whole different story. We went in to see our accommodations. It was all cement, and our room had a yellow pool of water on the floor dripping from a water spot on the ceiling. A large cockroach ran across the floor. Sandye screamed!

> Sandye: "Awwwwww, Ughhhh! I can't live like this. We must go home. This is not what Jack described. I will go home and dig ditches before I can live like this."

So, we went to Brenda. She was laying outside on a chase lounge sunning in a tiny bikini with her new friend Robert.

> Sandye: "Brenda, we are going to go home. I'm not spending a winter in a pigsty, treated like second class citizens."

I think the way they treated the help was worse than the horrible accommodations. We felt degraded. Sandye was not going to put up with that. Brenda, on the other hand, had a new beau chasing after her, and she was going to stay with Robert. We left and went back to Hilton Head. We did get part time jobs with the Hoar Construction company helping to build the Islands new mall. That helped during the low tourist season.

After the first Winter season Brenda moved back to Hilton Head with Robert, and the girls were once again attached at the hip. The four of us spent lots of time together. One time we decided to make up a new game which caught on with the rest of the employees at the Crazy Crab. We met at the Holiday Inn Tiki Bar with our "Pee Wee Herman fat tire Beach Bikes." Another friend of ours brought an old pick-up truck. There were about twelve participants. Jared was a friend who loved to party on Saturday and then attended church on Sunday. The idea of barhopping was especially appealing to him.

Hilton Head had about twenty-five premiere golf courses on a twelve-mile Island, but they had never seen a golf course like we created. This was our new game called bar golf. We had an initial drink at the Tiki Bar, and I screamed:

Kent: "It's now time to go to hole 2."

The group screamed: "HOLE 2!"

So off we went down the beach headed to the next closest bar. Sandye and Brenda lead the misfit bunch on bikes down this beautiful stretch of Hilton Head Island beaches. After three drinks "or should I say 3 holes", we headed inland to get on the bike paths and head for a bar called Shuckers. Rob drove our pace pick-up truck behind, carrying anybody that didn't feel like pedaling their bike to the next hole/Bar. Our goal was to get through 9 holes. After drinking another drink at the 4th hole and doing a bonus Jello shot, we were feeling no pain. At least six of us sat on top of our bikes in the truck and started off to the 5th designated mapped out bar. As we pulled away, one of the girls said:

Marcia: "Hey, Marty's bike is on this truck but where is Marty?"

The old truck was pulling away with the music blasting inside. Before reaching full speed, out of the restaurant comes Marty running full speed yelling:

Marty: "Hey wait for me!"

This became a great challenge. Marty was in great shape, and he was bound and determined not to be left behind. Rob, the driver, was having fun with the two people up front and was oblivious to what was transpiring in the back.

Group in the back: "Go Marty, Go Marty, you can do it."

We were laughing and screaming. Just as the truck was about to pull away, Marty, running as fast as he could, made a huge leap and landed in the back of the truck on top of the pile of bikes. The group sitting around could not have been louder, screaming like we had won the Olympics of bar golf. I am sure that Marty was cut up from landing on those bikes, but he was proud of showing off those game wounds. We did not make it to nine holes, but our goal of total fun was reached after hole or should I say bar number six. Everyone had dispersed and I remember, Sandye, Brenda, Robert and I riding our bikes about two blocks back to our homes. We were worn out with smiles on our faces, trying to keep the bikes up and not falling off or into a ditch. Those were great times with no worries. We could not maintain that kind of lifestyle but for the time being it was great to be young and falling in love.

My compulsive behavior backfired on me when my gambling addiction put a huge setback in our relationship. We had been saving for a trip to Spain to visit her friend, Avril and her husband, Jose. Sandye contacted Avril with the news that the trip was on, and joy filled both rooms. She didn't know that I gambled the money away and was in big trouble with a bookie. I think that facing Sandye was far worse.

Sandye: "You did what?"

Kent: "The money's gone. I lost it."

My first instinct from the past was to leave and never come back. I thought that I had destroyed another relationship. Sandye called as I was trying to get out the door.

Sandye: "Wait a minute. You stay right here and we are going to deal with this situation right now. You have to call Avril and tell her that we can't come."

That call was humbling and one of the hardest things I ever had to do. Sandye looked forward to seeing her friend and my reckless behavior ruined it for both of them. I thought more about myself than I did for them. Sandye could have sent me reeling but she didn't. We never talked to them again. Sandye never forgot. She still longed to see them someday. Chuck, the owner of the restaurant bailed me out with the bookie. I knew I needed help and started attending a twelve-step program for gambling addicts. Sandye should have left me at that moment. She must have seen something in me that I didn't. Instead, she supported my recovery and stayed right beside me as I wanted to change but had know idea how to do it.

***

Chip, chip, chip. My destructive gambling habit needed to be removed. Sandye also kept us from impending peril, and I needed to know how she did that. I never knew true friendship like the girls enjoyed or how to be flexible when situations arise. The fun-loving side of me was great but I needed balance in my life. The final masterpiece needed more positive qualities.

Three Month Trip

The next Winter we had to make new plans. We decided, after saving a healthy sum over the summer and fall, to travel the country. It was nineteen eighty-nine. We figured that if we could get along for months traveling in a car without killing each other, then this relationship just might work out. Sandye's Oldsmobile Firenza was loaded for the trip. We traveled north and enjoyed the rich history in Washington, DC. Those memories fueled future visits, especially over Veterans Day. Memories included huge shrimp cocktails at the Union Train Station and the view from a restaurant high above everything. There we joyfully watched all the people scurrying for the trains like little ants below us. On one occasion, while visiting monuments downtown, a veteran in a wheelchair approached the wall at the Vietnam Veterans Memorial with all those names of fallen soldiers that seemed to go on forever. The man took a coin and pressed it against a napkin and scrubbed a fellow fallen warrior's name onto the napkin. He then rolled his wheelchair back, paused and saluted. Tears flowed down Sandye's cheeks. We were proud to be Americans and wish everyone could feel what we were experiencing. Visiting all the Monuments and the Arlington Cemetery, where the tomb of the unknown soldier was located, made a lifetime impression on both of us.

After leaving DC with warm memories, we headed to Niagara Falls. We stayed in a little quaint hotel with a heart shaped bathtub that looked out onto the incredible waterfalls. We could see the American side through the falls. The Canadian side was spectacular. We went on a tour and wore the supplied yellow raincoats. We took an elevator down and then a rock stairway led us right behind the waterfalls. The water was roaring so loud you could scream and no one would hear you. Everything seemed magical as the water was misting and covering us. We will never forget that moment.

After returning to the States, we headed down to Pennsylvania, stopping to see her father. He lived two hours north of Pittsburgh. His name was Aldo Tarsisius Pietropoli. He was a full-blooded Italian and very passionate about everything. When he saw Sandye, he hugged her like he had not seen her his whole life. Sandye felt his strong embrace. Although he was only five foot seven, his presence seemed so big that when he entered the room he commanded your attention. He shook my hand and sized me up. He didn't know if I was going to be a fling for his daughter or a keeper. We had a good time spending Thanksgiving with him. He knew how to be a host, which Sandye learned from both her mother and father. While growing up, Sandye went to church three times a week. He was a very religious man who never missed an opportunity to share his faith. These conversations were all foreign to me and I couldn't wait to leave. Sandye had not attended church since she was eighteen, and I had no interest either. It was time to go.

We headed down to see Sandye's old stomping grounds in Charleston, West Virginia. We began to have car trouble, so we stayed at her old girl-friend's house for a week while the car was being repaired. We went for a walk up a path as snow was falling. We looked down over this winding river with snow everywhere. The city in the background looked like a Hallmark Postcard. We soaked in the moment and loved on each other. I did find my way to the Dog Track. I won but had to go right back to gamble more and lost the money I won plus more. This pattern always repeated itself. It had been about a month since we left and it was time to head west.

We drove to Denver for Christmas with my family. My whole family drank and smoked pot a lot. This was no exception. We joined right in the middle of the party scene just like I had always learned.The focus for Christmas was presents and no one went to church. I did get to take Sandye up to the Great Rocky Mountains and tried to show her how to ski. It was a huge lesson. Just because you know how to do something doesn't mean you know how to teach someone that task. Sandye was on skis way up the mountain, mad and scared with no way out, she started screaming at me.

> Sandye: "Why did you bring me up here? Now I am stuck and cannot get off this mountain." (As the skis were moving below her feet and she kept falling to the ground)

Then I had an idea.

> Kent: "Okay, let me get behind you. I can pull you up and put my ski's outside of yours. We can start going down the hill together as one."

So, with no other choice, other than call the Ski Patrol for help, she conceded to try. I then lifted her up, wrapped my arms around her waist and with her ski's inside of mine started to go down the hill. At first, she was nervous, but when she realized that we were going down the hill and I had complete control, moving back forth on the mountain with a smooth rhythm. It took her a few minutes to trust that she was safe, and I had complete control.

Sandye: "Hey we're doing it. This is ok. This is fun!"

We laughed and enjoyed every moment going down that hill. Once we got to the bottom, she requested a ski instructor for a real lesson. That was the first and last time that she went snow skiing.

Then on to Las Vegas, where she met my mother who now lived there. She was now selling Real Estate and doing well, but still wild and looking for a man to define her. I could see why my life was all over the place and disjointed. We stayed with mom for New Years with big festivities on the Las Vegas Strip, including fireworks. By the time we started back and stopped again in Denver for a week, the weather was below zero. Sandye caught the flu and needed time to recover. I realized that both places we lived in before, West Virginia and Denver, were great memories but were not the same. We were becoming different people, and it was time for us to grow, change and find a new direction together. On our way back the next stop was New Orleans, where we only planned to stay one day. We loved it so much that we stayed a week. We visited the Super Dome. It hosted a Carnival with rides that took us up to the ceiling of the dome.

We visited all the local places and Sandye taught me to eat oysters on the half shell. We had a grand time seeing the authentic side of New Orleans. Our money ran out and we headed home. The trip lasted three months. I knew I had found my best friend. We shared the same dreams. We both loved to travel. We were compatible. Three months together seeing this beautiful country with a special person made me realize that I did not want to live without her. I also knew that I had much to learn.

Sandye would give away things on a whim, while I would gamble them away without a thought of helping someone else. Her giving spirit was infectious. I knew that I had to show more compassion. We both wanted the best for each other. Her giving stemmed from her childhood. Each Christmas, her father told his children to give away a wrapped present to a stranger without first opening it. I saw her raise money for families with needs and I loved that about her. Just as she tried to instill passion in me, she lived it. On Hilton Head she decided that she wanted to get everyone at the Boys and Girls Club a present.

> Sandye: "Look at the twenty-five names on this list. They don't name their kids simple names like John and Sue anymore." (as she chuckled)

She thoughtfully picked out each present for every child. This was the first time I had seen her do such a selfless thing without wanting anything in return. I helped, watched and started to learn it wasn't always about me.

***

Chip, chip, chip. For me holidays were about receiving gifts and having fun. Sandye introduced the concept of giving sacrificially. Selfishness needed to be removed and replaced with heartfelt compassion. Enjoying fellowship with that special person went well beyond my fun-loving experiences of the past.

Back to School

In nineteen-ninety we returned from our three-month trip and moved to the Marshside Apartments on the northside of the island. Sandye and Brenda now joined me working at the Crazy Crab. We loved Christmastime, although, I did not fully understand what the season truly meant.

I previously attended college for five years in Colorado. I still needed about a year and a half to graduate. Obviously, I did not use my time wisely in school. For example, I could never get up in time for a language class, which I dropped every year. While taking classes in Beaufort, I enrolled in the psychology of marriage class. There were some older people who had been married for a substantial amount of time in the class. Those people and the professor made a hard stand on the topic of being married over living together. They said that you were taking your relationship to another level in marriage. I argued strongly that my three-year relationship was as committed as their marriage and that I did not need to get married. They said, "just wait and see." Although I was very adamant, I would recall their words later with a rude awakening.

After saving up enough money, we put a down payment on our first condo. It was a block from the Coligny Beach near where we initially lived. When you opened the windows at night you could hear the ocean waves in the distance. We were officially homeowners. It was very comfortable and the area was familiar. Now we needed to get focused. Sandye was supportive and encouraged me go back to college to finish my degree. I started commuting forty-five minutes to take classes twice a week, while I was working with Sandye at the Crazy Crab the other days.

On my twenty-eighth birthday, she surprised me with a party at our condo. She was wearing a white T-Shirt with a fish painted on it and had a party hat on. The shirt said: "Kent's Brim and Bass Birthday Bash." People started showing up and, to my surprise, all twenty-five of them were wearing that shirt, which she designed with her friend Marcia from work. She arranged everything. We took a picture with me holding up a two-inch-long brim fish, caught in the pond behind the house with everyone around me. It was amazing. I froze that little fish for about a year before I finally departed with it.

She threw me another party for my twenty-ninth birthday. This time our coworkers knew how great Sandye could host a party. Way too many people showed up for our little place to accommodate. Many of them had a newer version of the same shirt from the previous year. While Sandye was upstairs waiting in line for the bathroom, the police were called because of the noise. Feeling no pain I asked the police:

Kent: "Why did you come?"

Policeman #1: "Why do you think we came?"

Kent: "Because you wanted to wish me a Happy Birthday?" (smiling)

Everyone laughed, even the Police snickered.

Policeman #2: "Okay, Happy Birthday, but some of these people might be underage, and if we have to come back it won't be a Happy Birthday."

They left. Sandye came down and missed the whole thing. Once she found out the police were called, she abruptly ended the party and sent everyone home. She said that next year we would have to do something different. I still had a great time because of the work she did to pull off that party.

While I attended school, Sandye completely renovated the condo by herself. She also enjoyed landscaping and made the view from the street beautiful as well. She knew how to make a house a cozy home.

Robert and Brenda decided to get married. Brenda asked Sandye to be her Maid of Honor. They selected Brenda's childhood home in the Poconos in Pennsylvania for the wedding. The four of us represented Hilton Head. Jarod had moved back to Wisconsin the year before but enjoyed coming to big events. On the wedding day, Jarod and I were enjoying a beer while watching little league baseball on the TV in the hotel. The wedding party left early for the four-o'clock wedding. Jarod and I were laughing and realized that it was three-thirty; we might be late. My sense of punctuality was still awry. My mother was the same way. By the time we arrived the wedding had just started. We slipped into one of the rows as the wedding march was playing.

Robert was up in the front with the pastor and Sandye was on her way down the aisle. As she passed me, she gave me a look to kill. Then Brenda came down the aisle with her father and looked beautiful. The ceremony was perfect and the full sit-down dinner followed. It was a traditional wedding with over a hundred and fifty people. My tardiness was soon forgotten when the whole crowd started doing the chicken dance. This bonded Sandye and Brenda so much closer. Shortly afterwards, the couple decided to move to Robert's hometown in Sarasota, Florida. Brenda and Sandye vowed to stay very close friends and celebrate as many big events as possible together every year.

To fully understand Sandye, I needed to get to know the people who were significant in her life. Her best friend was Brenda who became closer than a sister. She was an ex-marine. Sandye changed her stoic behavior to be more flexible. They often wore the two shirts made that identified them as joined at the hip. One said, "BB1" for Blonde Bombshell #1. The other said, "BB2" for Blonde Bombshell #2. Brenda would make the trip to Hilton Head about once a year or we would go to Florida to see them. During those visits, I knew that I was the odd man out. Sandye and Brenda would let Robert and I know when we could join them. They were best friends before I came into the picture. I knew my place and we always had fun. Robert was a great cook!

They missed each other so much that they started a tradition celebrating one another's birthday for an entire month. Brenda's was in October and Sandye's in May. At the beginning of each of those months they started mailing each other a pop-up birthday cake hat. No one else was allowed to wear the hat, although they tried. In addition, care packages would arrive on the first day of the month and each week that followed. Each birthday month became a festive and wonderful tradition year after year.

Sandye taught me a great lesson about giving, which initiated a Christmas tradition. After our three-month trip we bought each other high end gifts like leather coats, cowboy boots, and more. It was a good Christmas, but we spent six months paying off the credit cards. Something felt wrong. We decided to not buy gifts for each other on the next Christmas. Instead, we sponsored a needy family. It brought great pleasure to help somebody and share in their joy. We had a beautiful live Christmas tree without gifts beneath it, which felt like something was missing. We came up with a solution and went to the local thrift store with twenty dollars each. We took twenty minutes to purchase the most gifts for the money. Our tree had many presents that cost a total of forty dollars. I'll never forget the first present that I opened. It was a Mr. T Chia pet. The box said, "watch his mohawk grow." Sandye opened her gift with the $.99 price tag still on it.

Sandye: "Oh, honey. It's so nice. You shouldn't have spent so much." (laughed)

Kent: "I know that I outdid myself."

Sandye: "I must ask, 'What is it?'"

Kent: "I don't know. That's why I got it."

We spent the next thirty minutes guessing what it could be.

Sandye: "I think it's a life preserver."

Kent: "I think it's a hemorrhoid pillow."

We never knew what it was, but we had a ball.

What a relief to not have expectations and spend a joyful time together while helping families in need. We knew that most of these items would be returned for resale. We named this tradition, "Twenty-twenty," which meant twenty dollars and twenty minutes.

One morning, Sandye was looking at the local paper, The Island Packet. She noticed an article about an upcoming rally to be held in Beaufort, S.C. This was a march/parade supporting the KKK. Sandye was raised near a very poor area that mostly supported her father's business (all-purpose convenient store). She strongly believed in equality for all people as I did.

Sandye: "I can't believe my eyes. Is this 1992 or are we in the fifties? Can you believe this?"

Then she held the paper up, pointing at the article.

Sandye: "They're not going to get away with this. I am going to this march to protest."

Once she made her mind up, there was no going back. On the day of the march, while I was working, she went there with a friend. He was a huge man whom we called "Big Chuck." He was big but soft as a teddy bear. She told me that as the march passed by, she held up a sign that read, "See with your heart, not with your eyes." One of the KKK leaders, in a green mask and robe, (grand master) came right up to her.

KKK Leader: "Lady. You don't know what we're about."

Sandye held her sign firmly above her head.

Sandye: "Take your mask off. I can't hear you."

The man locked eyes with her and she did not back down. He let out a big groan and marched away. She turned around and saw "Big Chuck" had run back behind a building and hid. He never heard the the end of that as we joked about him being there as Sandye's bodyguard. Sandye stood up for her beliefs of what is right or wrong. It defined her. She didn't care about the danger when she knew she needed to make a stand.

On my thirtieth birthday, Sandye only bought two new customized shirts. She said that we were going to Brunswick Georgia for a weekend to celebrate, this time foregoing the big parties and the police. As we were driving through Savannah, she said:

Sandye: "Don't you want a Bloody Mary for your Birthday?"

It was 11am on a Sunday. We were near the airport.

Kent: "Well, the only place that I can get a drink this early is the airport. Why don't we stop there?"

She agreed with my idea, and I came to a stop in the parking lot.

Sandye: "I accidentally left the recycle bag in the trunk, would you get that out?"

Kent: "Why would you put the recycle in the trunk?"

Sandye: "We were on the way out and I didn't want to leave it for the weekend, would you get it please?"

I opened the trunk and to my surprise, balloons flew with confetti and there was a packed suitcase.

Sandye: "Get the bags and let's go get your Bloody Mary."

I was in shock, while following her around the airport, with her not telling me anything that was going on. After getting that drink, we went to a terminal, where she shaded my eyes as we boarded a plane. I still did not know where we were going. Sandye had a talk on the side with the flight attendants. Two hours later I heard the flight attendant on the intercom: "Welcome everyone, especially Kent on his thirtieth birthday, to Cancun, Mexico."

Wow! I couldn't believe it. Sandye brought seconds on all my clothes and a new docket kit with a shaver and toothpaste. I thought we were going for two nights to Brunswick Georgia, but three hours later I was swimming under a waterfall drinking out of a coconut in Mexico on the most beautiful beach. We partied and snorkeled for a week. She took care of everything. It was the thought and the love that was so amazing. I was hooked forever.

***

Chip, chip, chip. The sculpturer steps back to view his creation and hopes to see signs of life. Slowly, the act of giving begins to take hold of my heart. My lack of discipline begins to improve as all of this misguided energy is starting to get focused towards something more meaningful. Small things like the twenty-twenty celebration and big events like Sandye's surprise birthday trip become extra special. Love grows deeper.

The Diagnosis

Sandye's health began to take a turn. She knew something was wrong and started to seek professional help. She went to a hospital in Charleston, S.C. where she met Dr. Tyre. Her vision was impaired, and it frightened her. Dr. Tyre diagnosed it as optic neuritis and assured her that she was not going blind.

Dr. Tyre: "Sandye, you have multiple sclerosis (MS)."

Sandy: "What does that mean?"

Dr. Tyre: "You are not going blind. Your muscles are losing strength."

When Sandye left the hospital, she was crying. It grieved my soul.

Kent: (not knowing what to say) "It's going to be alright."

Sandye: "I am not crying because of MS. Just the opposite."

Kent: "What do you mean?"

Sandye: "I'm crying because I am not going blind. I can deal with MS. I know what to expect." (She was crying because she was actually relieved. She found the positive side of getting MS as a better choice than not going blind.)

The trip home was filled with mixed emotions. We discussed future plans. I knew that I had to earn my degree and secure a better paying position to support both of us. After a grueling two years in college, I managed to get to the end but still negotiated some grades with professors. I was always out to get more than I deserved. I was able to graduate in 1992. My mom attended with her new boyfriend Jelindo Angelo (J.A.). I finally completed something that I started. It was a struggle. I was also enrolled in a group called, "Leadership Hilton Head." This was a high-powered program with top businessmen in the area participating in non-profit and educational learning. It was also a way for me to meet the heavy hitters in business there. To finish this program, I had to complete a personal project. As usual, I was behind and overcommitted. As in the past, I would try to solicit help from others. Sandye was adamant to not help or allow anyone else to get involved. I was angry for not getting my way but loved her for building discipline in my work environment.

After I graduated we were back working very hard in the middle of a double shift. Sandye and I took a break and sat down at the Crazy Crab bar. I now had my first opportunity for a businessman's real job at Coastal Food Distributors. Although, this job did not require a degree. I called and got an interview. That opened the door for a second and third interview. They offered me the job. It entailed selling groceries for a distributor directly to Hilton Head restaurants. For the first time I was uncertain if I would be able to handle this job and needed to share my feelings with Sandye.

Kent: "They offered me the position. I'm not sure if I am cut out to do this job."

Sandye: "Oh, you're capable and you can do it. Just take one thing at a time, handling whatever is right in front of you first. Use your great personality and your hard work. Show them who you really are."

I never forgot those words and never looked back. I left the restaurant and started working at Coastal Foods. I began selling their products to various restaurants where I worked prior. I went through formal training for basic business fundamentals. The sales structure was commissioned based, which added fuel to my competitiveness. When corporate meetings were held, Sandye knew that I enjoyed the limelight and offered her words of wisdom.

Initially, I started with a salary, but soon afterwards they put me on straight commission. That was a huge boost in my earnings as I won multiple gross profit awards with the company. My restaurant ties became large customers. The owners of the Crazy Crab where I worked supported me and rewarded me with substantial business. I undersold my competition, but my sales volume was several times higher than my nearest competitor. I went through formal training for basic business fundamentals. Sandye saw how I dealt with my customers and provided constant encouragement. She knew that customers respected me and that I looked out for their best interests. That was a combination that launched my career. When my competition sold cases of ketchup for $27 a case, I sold it for $22, while still making a profit. I loved the feeling of seeing my customer's reactions. Sales was what I did well and it was fulfilling.

Sandye was able to get around that year but had to limit any strenuous work. On one occasion we met a woman named Dianne at the Crazy Crab Restaurant. Dianne was eating mussels (a local seafood delight) at the bar.

Sandye: "My name is Sandye. Is it okay if I sit here?"

Dianne: "Sure. I would love the company. My husband travels a lot."

Sandye: "Kent works a lot too."

Dianne: "Larry is rarely home. Work takes him all over the world."

Sandye: "That must be tough. At least Kent comes home to sleep in his bed at nights."

Dianne: "Larry is a great provider, but I miss him terribly."

Sandye: "I'm available any time you need to talk."

Dianne: "Thank you. I would love that."

That started a longtime friendship. Dianne had a huge heart and laugh that would stop the whole room in its tracks. She couldn't wait to tell her husband about Sandye. When Larry finally got to meet us at the bar, I was involved in a bizarre contest at an outdoor food festival on the island. I was one of the final four who had to race with a tray full of wine-filled glasses. On this occasion, I tripped. The wine spilt everywhere including on some of the spectators. My first impression to Larry was not a good one.

A couple of years later after Larry learned about Sandye's MS, the first impression from a business man's perspective was replaced with one filled with respect. I found that out later as they stayed in constant touch. We only knew them for a few months before they moved away. Still, Dianne would call Sandye and talk often.

When corporate meetings were held, Sandye knew that I enjoyed the limelight and offered her words of wisdom.

> Sandye: "Please don't put the lampshade on your head and try to stay under the radar."

It took me years and years to slowly change. Let's say that I am still working on that, lol.

Hilton Head was very seasonal for business. From April until October was the high time. When they sponsored contests to win a trip, I was focused to win. One of these included a trip to Disney World on the Concierge floor at the Swan hotel. Seeing this opportunity, Sandye looked me in the eyes and said:

> Sandye: "I want to go to Disney World with you. You have got to win this."

That was all I needed to hear. I made my own sales book with all the products listed. On a visit to one of the restaurants, I learned to not make any assumptions. After taking their regular order, I showed them my Disney World book but failed to show the breakfast section. The manager said:

Manager: "Hey. What about those items?"

Kent: "Those are breakfast items."

Manager: "I'll take thirty cases of the sausage links and thirty cases of the liquid eggs."

Kent: (After being blown away) "You don't even serve breakfast."

Manager: "I cater to a church once a month and I want to help you."

I never made assumptions after that and won one of the top three awards. That put us on the concierge floor with all the extras. Boy, was Sandye happy. I found a way to sell high volumes at low prices and still make the most profit. When the golf tournaments came to Hilton Head, I won the catering contract orders, which was big business. One of the perks with the restaurant at the golf course was the manager took me out to play a round at the Heritage Golf Course where the annual professional tournament is played. I felt like I was actually fitting into the business world.

Every customer needed to be met at a scheduled time, and I was not good at keeping those meetings. But my customers enjoyed my company or were at least amused by me and helped me succeed. They realized that I wore my heart on my sleeve and that I was genuine and my actions heartfelt. I learned that when all things are equal, customers will choose to purchase from people that they like and trust. I found a way around the structured system to succeed and make a living. One boss told me that when I didn't like the rules, I would change the game and it was fun. My customers still enjoyed the experience despite and because of my delinquent behavior.

The successful results came through my passion for my customers, especially when they needed something fast. For example, a chef on the beach made a huge error and missed the weekend's order time. If I didn't help him they would be out of food for the weekend. I purchased a used ford mustang convertible from a friend at the restaurant. (Sandye insisted that my classic van needed to finally be put to rest, plus the convertible was cool so I was OK with that) I drove for an hour-and-a-half from the corporate office back to the Island with the top down. It was the only way I could carry all the groceries needed by my customer. As I was driving back to Hilton Head, it started to rain. The cases were wet, but still held together. There were four forty-pound boxes of crab legs. The chef was overjoyed. He didn't care about the wet cases. I made a huge commission on that order. After we sold the car, I spotted it six months later. I approached the owner and told him that I used to own that car. After I asked him how he liked it, he said, "It's a great car but there was always a BAD smell coming from the back seat that I could not get rid of." I told him that it was from crab legs, and I apologized while trying not to laugh.

While I was working, Sandye was making our new home a beautiful haven. She was spending a lot of time helping Dianne totally renovate their new home in the Sea Pines Plantation, which was where Harbourtown was located. Sandye and I played with their twin grandbaby girls on their living room floor and belly laughed with Dianne about life.. Larry was off in the world running a large company. At this time Sandye started experiencing stomach pains. She said that she knew what they were. We went to the doctor, and she needed to have a cyst removed from around her ovaries.

Sandye: "This was a chronic problem and was about the fifth

cyst over the years that needed removing dating back to 1980. In the early 80's the first one that the doctors discovered almost took my life. When the doctors removed that cyst, it was the size of a football."

I was in shock and could not believe this was happening. Sandye on the other hand was calm and told me not to worry. She had an inner strength and a history of fighting for her life that relaxed her in the toughest of situations. I had no idea how I would need her strength through our lives.

Sandye: "So, this is a small cyst that they need remove now. It will be a piece of cake."

I know she did not want to scare me, for this was all new to me. I proceeded to watch her go through three cyst surgeries over the next couple of years, which was the first time that I spent time in the hospital overnight. Back then, doctors would cut into her belly and remove the cyst. This meant she had to stay in the Hospital at least two days.

I remember witnessing the third surgery. We rushed to the hospital because she was in severe pain. Sandye knew that she would not be able to take a shower for at least a week after the surgery. With the urgency to get to the hospital, she did not have time to take a shower. We were in the hospital room.

Kent: "They are about ready to come and get you to go down to surgery."

I was thinking that we would have a few quiet words together.

Sandye: "Quick! I am going to lean back into the shower. You can quickly wash my hair."

Kent: "What, NOW! They will be coming any minute to get you."

Sandye: "I am not going a week or two with this dirty hair, now get the shampoo and hurry."

I found the shampoo they provided, and she tipped back, I ran the shower over her hair only trying not to get her hospital gown wet. Sandye was very focused like she had done this before.

Sandye: "Put a lot of shampoo on your hands and clean my hair."

I was vigorously lathering up her hair, right as the door of the hospital room came flying open. Three attendants came in with a bed to take her down to surgery. They looked at her, and Sandye looked up like she was caught with her hand in the candy jar.

Attendant 1: "What on earth are you doing?"

Attendant 2: "We need to take you to surgery right now the doctor is waiting in the operating room."

Sandye: "My hair was dirty, and I had to clean it first." (she sounded like a little girl)

Having no choice, they knew they could not take her downstairs in her present condition.

> Attendant 1: "All right, were going right out in this hallway, and we are going to wait. This better be the fastest shower you ever took, or you will miss your surgery."

They went back out in the hallway and waited. The second the door was closed. Without missing a beat, Sandye dropped the little girl look and went to work.

> Sandye: "Okay, here's our chance. Let's take care of business. Get me clean and smelling good."

We hurried, washed, cleaned, and dried her hair. Then I let the attendants, who were not too happy, back into the room to take her down. I wondered what they were telling the doctors and staff as to why they were having to hold up the operating room. I knew it was not right to do that and felt bad, but it was comical after the fact. After the surgery it took four or five days to leave the hospital. Sandye looked at me with a wry smile as if to say, "I am so glad my hair is clean while I lay here in pain." I also learned that I needed to be focused on her needs and be an advocate for her in the hospital. There were many times she needed me to be strong and stand in the gap for her when she couldn't and if I didn't help her when she desperately needed it, her life could be compromised. This was a personality trait that I had to develop strength for.

At the last minute on Valentine's Day in nineteen-ninety-three, I stopped at the local Kroger's store to buy a gift. A large chocolate chip cookie caught my eye, and I brought it home. Planning ahead was not one of my skillsets and this day I learned a valuable lesson.

Kent: "Happy Valentine's Day, Sandye."

Sandye: "Don't you ever do that again, mister."

Kent: "Do what?"

Sandy: "You need to plan in advance, especially on special occasions. No more last minute big cookies or foot messagers (like I previously got for her from Walgreens when it was the last store open)."

She was right. My carefree upbringing did not include any forethought. Spur of the moment decisions were common. After that episode, I began thinking well ahead and started saving to meet a goal. I put an emerald ring on layaway and surprised her with it a year later. I asked a chef in a high-end restaurant to place the ring in a dessert he made special for the occasion. It was a gift that warmed her heart. Then I knew that I was now on the right track putting all my creative energy to be more considerate in the future. Sandye was always coming up with surprises that should have taught me to do the same for her. I guess it took a cookie to convince this airhead.

Sandye's Italian background showed up with her great cooking skills. Coming home each night for dinner was a special treat. Although she started to lose some muscle strength, those times in the kitchen gave her pleasure. She was skilled in the preparation and knew when to rest. It also gave her a sense of fulfillment, since she was unable to work full time. It also put the pounds on me. It was a good thing that I enjoyed running.

After three years of selling food at Coastal, the company had a big promotion to sell Minute Maid juice machines to our customers. If the customer bought the juice, the machine was free. Minute Maid sent several representatives to ride with selected salesmen from Coastal. They provided an incentive to the sales rep for each machine sold. I was fortunate, that the regional manager named, Pamela Cervenka, rode with me. Every account that we visited received a machine. We led the company in placements. I received a large bonus check from Minute Maid because of that promotion. Pam and I really clicked in personality and seemed to thrive off each other's passion. Shortly after, Pam called me and said they had an account manager's position open in Atlanta and asked if I was interested in coming there for an interview. This was an unconventional move for a company to pull another company's rep to work for them. I have not heard of another distributor rep moving to another manufacturing company. It's unheard of in that business. So, I went to Atlanta for the interview. Afterwards, they offered the position to me. I didn't think it was up my alley, but I went home that night to discuss it with Sandye.

Kent: "I got a new job offer today, Sandye."

Sandye: "Tell me about it."

Kent: "It involves a move to Atlanta. What do you think?"

Sandye: "What will you be doing?"

Kent: "More Sales but the company is huge. They are owned

by Coca Cola."

Sandye: "I'm sure they will help with the move."

Kent: "That's for sure."

Sandye: "You should take it."

Kent: "Are you sure?"

Sandye: "We need to go."

There was something about her sense of urgency that told me she was right. I called Pam and accepted the position. I was not sure about leaving the islands but knew that Sandye's intuition was not to be ignored.

While I was gone, unbeknownst to me, Sandye, for the first time in nineteen years, prayed to God that I would get this job. Her father had taken them to church three to five days a week until she was eighteen. All of his children stepped away from the church after leaving home. (Later she told me that it was because she felt tied down and wanted to be free from the hard pressure to go to church) She knew to come back to the Lord because of her childhood experiences. At that time she also was trying to complete her college degree and made the decision to drop out, sell the condo, and move to Atlanta when I was offered the position. She loved school and leaving it for our benefit was one of the hardest things she ever had to do. I did not understand this kind of love until years later. As we were leaving the island, I did have dreams of asking her to marry me but could not get it all together to do that. I was aware of her bad divorce history and was unsure that she would say yes.

I had one more incident with gambling, like a self-destructive mode when things were going well. Chuck, the manager/owner of the Crazy Crab, talked to the bookie and worked out a deal for me. I now was moving into that official business position where I carried a credit card, took customers to lunch, and enjoyed having people wait on me. I now thought I was "the big cheese" and special, but deep down I was scared to death.

We spent eight years on Hilton Head Island, which became a premier resort destination from across the world. It was a great time. Families come to the island to enjoy golf, restaurants, bars and many beaches. It is a great place to visit and have fun. All my friends and relatives came to the island to play. Many of the people that I worked with had college degrees and came there to get away from society. There was excess in every disfunction. I lost friends who drank too much, drove in the water and drowned. I will forever remember the great times that we had but knew that it was time for a new life in a city that had culture and stability.

***

Chip, chip, chip. My strong work ethic and customer care began to open new doors of opportunity. I knew that to care for Sandye's needs in the future, I had to be a better provider. Exposure to her medical issues also became a challenge. A lack of trust in my abilities was holding me back. I needed to believe in myself. Sandye's inner spirit began to lead her in prayer directed towards me. The artist used Sandye to teach me many lessons about life and things of the heart. Gambling still had its grip on me. Learning about Sandye's MS changed everything.

Wedding Bells in Georgia

Everything was fresh and new after arriving in Atlanta. Our first three months were spent at the Homewood Suites Hotel. My boss, Pam, announced that I was a new employee on the company website. In the announcement, she stated that we were boyfriend and girlfriend. Sandye, having such a bad painful divorce, never wanted to get married again. With my mother married three times and working on her fourth, I wasn't ready either. When this announcement came out, Sandye's jaw dropped.

Sandye: "Now we are in trouble."

Kent: "What are you talking about?"

Sandye: "Now that I have progressive MS, we need insurance. We are not set up in the Coca-Cola system. I might not qualify for insurance moving forward. So, your boss has just forced us to get married by that announcement." (She always blamed Pam for that, which became a big joke for all of us.)

Kent: "You mean to tell me that we are going to get married for insurance?"

Sandye: "That's exactly what I am telling you."

My heart sunk a bit. I always knew that I wanted to ask her the traditional way with a special event. Her health and peace of mind was most important to me, and I would do anything to that end. So, we had to make it quick and have the announcement reposted as husband and wife. You could get a quick certificate of marriage in Tennessee. The next Friday we drove to Athens, Tennessee. That night, we had our rehearsal dinner alone at the Wendy's restaurant. The next morning, we went to the town magistrates' office and stood behind a couple who appeared as though they had been up all night. When it was our turn, the lady with the authority asked some quick questions and then asked Sandye if she would be my wife. Just wanting to have some fun with me, she replied:

Sandye: "Uh, I guess so."

Kent: "Sandye!" (While shaking her arm harshly)

Sandye gave me a sheepish grin. I knew she was having fun. Then they asked me the question, I said "I do", of course.

We went to the Waffle House for our wedding reception. The whole weekend cost under a hundred dollars. We have since laughed about the low cost of the wedding but deep down this troubled me because I really wanted it to be special. Over the next year, I made monthly layaway payments on a ring with two big diamonds and a blue topaz stone in the middle. I pulled up in front of the church and surprised her. I opened her car door and got down on one knee.

Sandye: "Why did you come here and what are you doing?"

Kent: "I wanted to do this for a long time and didn't get the chance. Now I'm doing it right. Would you please marry me and be my wife forever?"

Then I showed her the ring. She started crying a lot. You know that "ugly crying."

Sandye: (Through the tears) "Yes, of course I will."

Sandye was one of the only people in her family left in the United States that carried her last name forward (Pietropoli). She wanted to keep her last name and I respected that. Her father would always address us as the Cammack's but either way did not matter to me. So, I am Kent Cammak and she is Sandra Pietropoli the happily married couple!

While I worked, Sandye picked up items for our new home. We found a three-bedroom ranch style home in Lawrenceville, Georgia. As we pulled up to the house, a man across the street was playing baseball with his six-year old daughter. I rolled down the window and shouted.

Kent: "Hi. Do you live in that house?"

Russ: (with a feeling of doubt on his face) "Yes."

Kent: "My name is Kent, and this is Sandye. We're your new neighbors."

Russ: "Congratulations." (with a New England accent) "My
name is Russ."

He did not seem too excited.

I pulled into the driveway and told Sandye that Russ was a work in
progress. His personality had a negative first impression. As we got to know
Russ, his wife, Leslie, and their three children, we became very close. He
was an operations businessman working for General Electric, and their
go-to guy when anything went wrong in the plant. Every time that I needed
something repaired or constructed, we would make a project day together.
Russ would do the work, while I held the hammer and the beer. I knew my
limitations and they did not include that form of labor.

The Fourth of July and New Years became firework extravaganzas. The
first time we set off the fireworks, one drifted down onto an electrical wire.
It was no big deal, but Erin, their six-year-old daughter, started crying.

Erin: "Our house is going to burn down."

We laughed, while assuring her it was OK. Twelve years later, Erin would
dress herself up in camouflage, put black marks under her eyes and lead
the fireworks display. The oldest child Kyle was ten. At his first big event
at school, I tied his first tie. Their middle child Tim was so quiet that we
didn't know he existed for two years.

Sandye knew that it was time to start going to church. It had been
nineteen years for her, and I had only gone on a few Christmases. She
first took me to a Presbyterian church and then to a Methodist one. She
wanted one that was not overbearing for she did not want to scare me away
from church. We really liked the pastor at Mckendree United Methodist

Church in Lawrenceville. His name was Steve Dodson. After a few months attending the church, we invited Steve to our home. There we shared our background, and he sensed our uncertainty regarding the social aspects of the church. The stigma that church people were boring and didn't have fun was evident,

Steve: "Kent. Are you having fun at our church?"

Kent: "Yes. I hope to find some good friends there."

Steve: "Do you know that Jesus was a lot of fun?"

Kent: (shocked) "Oh, really?"

Steve: "Yes. Jesus was a party animal."

I looked at Sandye and together we couldn't believe that those words came from a pastor. I loved it and wanted to experience more. Everything I believed about church attendance was upside down. We attended regularly and our journey of faith began. We both accepted Christ as our Savior and followed up with the Methodist baptism ceremony. I began playing golf with Pastor Steve, which added about four hours of conversation in each round. During one round we were held up in a rainstorm and had time to talk.

Kent: "I am working to get ahead. I am not sure where that will lead me. I feel like I have a big purpose in life, perhaps a high business executive or something with an impact on a lot of people."

Steve: "God has you right where He wants you."

Kent: "How can that be, Steve? I feel like I have a larger purpose."

Steve: "Your job is to be Sandye's caregiver."

Kent: "I know that, and I love her so much that it's not really a job."

Steve: "People are watching you, Kent. You are doing God's work."

Kent: "I haven't thought about that. I just love her."

Steve: "The more people see that love in you, the more they see Jesus."

Kent: "Wow! That's deep."

Steve: "Just think how deep His love is for you and Sandye."

Kent: "You have really got me thinking now, Steve."

Steve: "Caring for Sandye, that's your ministry. That could be your purpose. You don't know how many people that will touch. Just keep listening to God."

The more we shared, the more I realized that Steve was right. God was in control. The messages from the pulpit in that Methodist church were great for me at the time but Sandye desired more. Feel good themes may have left attendees with a warm feeling that their lives were not so bad. Sandye's church experiences from her childhood stirred something inside her and now she wanted more than a surface relationship with Jesus.

We began to do many things with Russ, Leslie and their family. One day, we were at the table talking. Russ said that Leslie's fortieth birthday was coming up in two months and he wanted to do something special as a surprise. He said that he was not very good at this and had not done anything like this for Leslie before. He asked for help. Sandye, still physically able and knowing it would be tough, was excited. This was right in her wheelhouse.

Sandye: "Russ. If you trust me, I can plan this whole thing."

Russ: "Absolutely."

Over the next two months Sandye gave Russ a huge list of items to buy. Every three days, Russ would drop off a few items on the list. He invited her whole family down from Connecticut for a surprise birthday party. On the day of Leslie's birthday, Sandye worked her way struggling physically up the two flights of stairs to their second-floor kitchen. Leslie was working at a video store. Over the next four hours, Sandye performed her magic and cooked a dinner party for thirty people. At 6:30, all the people arrived with excited expectations. I looked at Sandye with food stains all over her apron. She looked as though she had been in a battlefield as she tried very hard not to show her fatigue from the MS. She had a big smile on her tired face. There was food everywhere. As Leslie came home from work, she pulled into the parking area under her house and came up the stairway to the kitchen. She smelled the Italian aroma throughout the house.

Leslie: "What's going on?"

The room erupted joyfully with "Happy Birthday, Leslie." She was blown away that her family was there and what her husband had done for her. They were not ones for tears but they flowed heavy from Leslie that night. Russ was not the type to pull something like this off. Later that night he told her that he could never have done it without Sandye. This night bonded the four of us even closer. This was the first time Russ realized that something was physically wrong with Sandye. Her fatigue was now showing but she covered it up well.

Humor Break

Another moment happened when Sandye was still driving. She still used the walker to help her maneuver to the car. After storing it in the trunk, Sandye would take the wheel and start it up. On this occasion, her legs were not responding as they should. She was able to put the car in reverse but had difficulty turning the wheel. It was as if the wheel was stuck. It turned the car horizontally across the lawn. Realizing the situation, she knew that she had to veer away from the tree while travelling down a steep hill. She was able to stop the car at the bottom of the hill on the grass. Seeing this from the next yard, our elderly neighbor moved at a crawl speed to the rescue. The steep incline got the best of him as he fell on his butt and slid down the grass. Now they were face to face laughing at each other. Pretty soon, they both found it difficult to stop. After I arrived home, I saw the tracks in the yard and knew Sandye was ok. I chuckled.

***

Sandye had to have a new cyst removed. This time the doctors performed a hysterectomy. During her recuperation, Sandye desired to get more involved with the church. After speaking with the pastor, she recognized the need to send cards to people going through difficulties with prayer concerns. This was a ministry initiated by Sandye that drew the church family into a closer relationship with her.

The Edgars were one family seeking prayer for their sick baby. The survival rate was very low for the child's illness. Sandye continued writing to many families as one way to serve in ministry. At the time I was fully focused on my work and did not realize her dedication to this card ministry. I remember a Sunday when Mr. Edgar held up his healthy son in church with pride. Sandye yelled.

> Sandye: "That's the Edgar baby. Thank God for his healing. I am so happy."

> Kent: "You know them?"

> Sandye: "I have been in prayer for their child and sending cards for a long time."

Sandye's joy was evident and the entire congregation shared the moment.

I understood that natural childbirth was not going to happen in our marriage. I loved children, but knew there would be other ways to satisfy this need. Sandye was heartbroken but accepted it. When people asked her about having children, she would joke that "we are child free."

***

Chip, chip, chip. Spirituality is introduced through church fellowship. The presence of God in my life helps me to see people as He does. Marriage is a commitment to each other and God. Life also needs times of humor as well. God introduces new friends as tools to cut away rough edges. The sculpture begins to show life.

Olympics

I was now back in the hospital room (2016, present time), and I was reliving our life one moment at a time. It was now 11:40 am. Sandye looked so pretty but asleep. I called my friend Steve.

> Kent: "Steve, please reach out to your son Pastor Dustin and have the church pray for God's will with Sandye, she is still incoherent and is in trouble." (As a tear ran down my face.)

> Steve: "I have reached out to our whole home group and people are praying in many states right now for her. I will call Pastor Dustin and give him the update. Hang in there. We love you."

As I hung up the phone, I tenderly kissed Sandye's forehead and prayed for her. As a coping mechanism my mind went back to home in Atlanta in 1995 where we were dreaming of our plight together. We had known each other for nine years now and there was lots of progress with the church and my jobs.

Working for Minute Maid was a great experience. My boss Pam and I got along well together. She challenged me to sell to all kinds of corporate customers out of my comfort zone. Regional divisions in three states cause me to travel. It was a great time to be in Atlanta working for a division of Coke-Cola. I always wore a suit and felt important when I went to their corporate office. I welcomed the opportunity to mature in my business acumen. My division was reorganized twice. I now had a new boss and Pam moved on.

The holistic doctor in Hilton Head said that once we got to Atlanta Sandye would now require more care from a neurologist. We found the best MS doctor in the southeast, if not one of the top five in the world. His name was Doctor William Stuart. He had a clinic in the Shepherd's Center in downtown Atlanta. The MS Center of Atlanta shared space with the group that treated paralyzed people. When we made the first visit, we saw all kinds of paralyzed people, which was difficult not knowing Sandye's future. At the time, MS was only being treated by steroids. They put Sandye through every test imaginable.

Dr. Stuart's assistant took Sandye down in the basement to see how far she would walk without tiring. She walked down a tunnel attached to Piedmont hospital. The walls were painted like a jungle, and she enjoyed going down there. Initially, she walked the entire way but each year afterwards, she tired early. We liked Dr. Stuart a lot. He wore a bow tie. Sandye would always say "Hello young man" to him and he would always smile. She was always upbeat and willing to try any treatment that would help her get better, all the while knowing that she had the slow debilitating progressive form of MS.

Dr. Stuart told Sandye that attitude was eighty percent of the battle, and she was on the right track. She asked him, privately, if she would continue to decline physically and what would be the best things for her to do to help her marriage. He told her that there might be a time when I would have to take physical care of her. While she was able, she could think of special things to do for me now. I would recall them later. Understanding this, Sandye started doing things at home to surprise me like making special dinners, romantic clothes that I never saw before, and other treats. Those visuals were crucial and are ingrained in my head even now.

On Sundays, we would go to church. Sandye had trouble maintaining her balance and would hold my arm so no one would notice. That worked for about a year. If she was by herself, she needed to use a cane for balance. When someone saw her later with a cane, they asked "What happened to you?" At that point she would let them know she had MS. One time when we were attending the symphony in downtown Atlanta, I parked in a handicapped area. She could not walk long distances due to fatigue. We had a handicapped tag on the rear-view mirror. I helped her out of the car, and we looked like a normal couple walking. It was still a struggle for her to get to the seat and back. When we returned to the car after enjoying the show, there was a note under the windshield wiper chastising us for using handicapped parking when other people needed it. If people only knew what we go through behind closed doors, they would be very different. That note bothered us a lot but also reminded me not to judge people by their appearance, as we have no idea what might be happening.

Sandye's family was very traditional on holidays. They spent a great deal of time laughing and cooking together in the kitchen. They shared the hard work for the big meals. My family rarely cooked and focused on activities like skiing. I helped Sandye cook Thanksgiving dinners since her family lived out of state. We invited my mother every year. While cooking we decided to stop every hour and share something we were thankful for. This became a tradition. We started putting each thankful thought on paper and placed them in a hat or bowl. We would stop whatever was happening to share what we were thankful for. I recall my nephew when he was twelve saying that he was thankful for his mother, which moved the whole room. This was a great tradition that we always reminisce about.

Humor Break

One day, Sandye started hearing scratching noises coming from below the house. There was no basement, only a tight crawl space about two feet high. Russ had a BB gun and began moving with me through the space to locate the source of the scratching. After nearly reaching the end, Russ let out a scream that may have caused the house to shake.

Russ: "UGH! Back, back, back..."

Kent: "What happened?" (both men scurried out from under the house as fast as they could)

Russ: "There's a Possum there."

Kent: "Where?"

Russ: "It was about a foot in front of my face and looking right at me."

Russ sprayed an anti-rodent chemical under the house and the possum was not seen again. We all laughed, although our knees took a beating crawling out.

***

Up until our marriage, my mom was not very cordial to Sandye. She barely spoke to her, I guess because nobody was good enough for her son. Once we were married, mom realized that the game had changed, and she needed to act differently.

She had been dating J.A. for several years and decided to get married. He was a well-established builder in Las Vegas, whose wife of fifty-years had passed away. He started his business with nothing and now was one of the most recognized people in Las Vegas. I really liked him, because of his faith and humble standards, even though he was worth millions. This was a huge score for my mother as he was the most eligible bachelor in the city. We flew out to their lavish wedding with all his adult children present.

At the reception, his oldest son said some words and asked if anyone from our side of the family would speak. I stood up. You could feel the tension in the air. Mom felt like an outsider coming into the family. I graciously welcomed their family into ours and offered a toast. As the sweat fell from my brow, I breathed a sigh of relief as everyone toasted and sat down. Later, mom was accepted into their Catholic church, which I hoped would change her faith, but did not. She was a Chameleon and did whatever it took to play the role. For example, she was a Democrat but celebrated with her husband at the Republican Convention for days. He was in his late seventies, and they travelled all over the world. She loved the fanfare and expensive things. He donated a million dollars to the UNLV. We pondered about all the good that she could have done with the money she was receiving from that marriage.

We attended a black-tie Andre Agassi event in Las Vegas, where J.A.'s company purchased three tables at ten-thousand dollars each. J.A. was a very benevolent man. All my siblings and Sandye were there. These were great times for mom, as she felt that she finally made it in life. Money and men defined success to her. I came back one more time to surprise mom on her sixtieth birthday. JA planned a special event in a private dining room at the Barbary Coast Casino. Mom's whole family was there. She almost passed out at the surprise. It was a great event, but it got the best of me. I stayed up all night gambling, while everyone went to sleep. My sister came walking through the casino around nine A.M. I saw her coming and walked away from the casino. I felt horrible that I had succumbed to my nemesis. I paid for it all day eating brunch and trying to stay awake. On the flight back, I was exhausted, beat up and prayed to God to change my habits. I knew that I had to do better in my job and helping Sandye down the road.

One time I rode with a national Coca-Cola service rep displaying my usual compassion and excitement. This lady said, "If you want to work your way up to a high level, you have to stop acting like it's your first day." I really had to think about her comment. I had to decide if I wanted to change who I really was. The fun-filled personality was my strong suit, which created an internal conflict within me. The Olympics were coming to Atlanta in 1996, and I was selected to represent Minute Maid on the Coca-Cola team. Coca-Cola had such a strong presence there, that some people in Atlanta were saying that it should be renamed, "The Coca-Cola Olympics." I helped roll out the new product, Soft Frozen Lemonade, all throughout the city prior to the games starting. I had a pass for Turner Field, where the Braves played, placing ice cream equipment throughout the complex. Turner Field held the opening ceremonies for the Olympics.

On that night, I had the privilege of working at the old Fulton County Stadium adjacent to the field. All the athletes were in this building before they walked down the carpet to Turner Field. Before the ceremony began, the crowd in Turner Field began doing the wave. At the same time, all the athletes joined in the wave as well. It was a joy being a part of that. The opening ceremonies lasted six hours. This gave me the chance to give Minute Maid products to athletes around the world, while meeting and hearing their stories. As the athletes lined up, there was a huge burst of excitement for each country. All the volunteers would cheer as each country passed by. Katie Couric passed by while conducting interviews only a few feet from me.

When the United States athletes approached, the tunnel became extremely loud from both the athletes and workers. There were over six-hundred athletes. As they started down the tunnel, the roar of "USA, USA" resounded through the building. It was louder than anything I had ever heard before. I was never prouder to be part of something so special. After the US entries passed, with the roar still at a fever pitch, the first "Dream Team," USA Men's basketball team, came down from the second level on a side ramp. That was an amazing moment. As we started to leave, the opening ceremonies were being broadcasted across the world. From our vantage point on the hillside, we could see the large TV screens inside Turner Field. Looking down towards the street, we watched the torch runner coming down the street from a block away and entered the stadium. The excitement was overwhelming as we wanted to see who would do the actual torch lighting for the USA. Mohammed Ali, with obvious Parkinson's disease, was shaking while struggling to light the torch. This moment touched the whole world. What an emotional moment!

My mother was in the stadium at the opening ceremonies. She found her way to Atlanta with a three-week reservation at the extended Stay Hotel. She wasn't going to miss a big event, especially when we lived in the host city. I always wondered why her now husband did not come. She didn't care. She enjoyed the highlife, spending exorbitant amounts of money. Once again, I couldn't help but think about how that money could better be used to help people in need. I am sure Sandye also felt those feelings about my mom but would show respect, love her and never say a word.

Brenda and Robert also came up during the festivities. We wanted to take them down to all the events but that there would be a lot of walking involved. This is when we realized that if Sandye was not going to miss anything, we needed a wheelchair for her to join us. I struggled learning how to push her in the wheelchair without knowing that there are right ways to do it. The first few times I pushed her in the chair was fine. Later, I accidently crashed into things. One time I was hurrying across the street and slammed into the curb. She almost flew out. Sandye would give me that look like "are you trying to kill me?" I learned a good lesson, that I needed to practice before facing different circumstances. Advanced planning was crucial.

Sandye's father wanted to visit. He drove down in his camper with his second wife of ten years (Sandye's mom had passed away fifteen years prior from cancer) to spend time with us and share his faith. I was now more accustomed to hearing about God. He was also a man who would repair something before replacing it with something new. He was raised up during the depression and served in WWII. He was a proud Italian American man. While raising Sandye, they would visit the Philadelphia museums carrying a brown bag lunch. He would also take his family to the Atlantic City beaches. We have a picture of Sandye, at three years old, building a sandcastle out of a paint bucket filled with sand. He owned a small convenience store next to a trailer park. Although he was stern, he was incredibly compassionate to all people. Now, I understood where Sandye's benevolence started. Although they had some rough patches, Sandye loved her father dearly.

In our Lawrenceville home, he was helping Sandye with her car in the driveway. As they were about to open the garage door, Sandye yelled:

Sandye: "Hit the button dad."

Dad: "No. We need to exit out the back door to save on

electricity. (which meant walking around the house to get into the car) You are spending your husband's money like a drunken sailor."

A couple days later I was in the kitchen with her father, and we needed to go outside through the garage, I hit the button for the garage door, and Pete followed me out with no comment. I guess because I was the man of the house, it was okay to spend money as I pleased. Sandye stood in the background shaking her head in disbelief at her father but not surprised at his actions. She witnessed his stubbornness in her childhood.

He was a proud man, and he praised God every day. His full name was, Aldo Tarsisiuis Pietropoli. We called him, "Pete." His family came to the United States from Sicily on a boat through Ellis Island by the Statue of Liberty, with only the items that they could carry. Pete was two years old at the time. We had a lot to be thankful for. One day while I was with him attempting to repair our master bathroom's toilet, he said: "We must get under the house to fix this. I knew what that meant. We crawled thirty feet on our hands and knees to the plumbing. He had the tools, and I had the flashlight.

Pete: "We need more parts from the store."

We crawled back out. I felt bad because he was seventy-eight years old. He wanted to do this out of love. After two more trips under the house, he said that we needed to go back to Home Depot one more time. His face dropped. I pleaded with him that I would get my neighbor to help.

Pete: "No. Not until the job is done."

I gained so much respect for him on that visit and was coming to love him. The repair was successfully completed.

***

Chip, chip, chip. Again, the sculptor steps back to see where improvements need to be made. Relationships needed to be improved, especially with family members. Visions of grandeur in the workplace need to be controlled. Compassion and patience continue to mold me. Special events, like the Olympics, instilled a strong sense of citizenship and respect.

Europe Get Away

Once we were married, knowing that Sandye had a progressive disease, we decided to fulfill every dream of traveling and make every journey a trip of a lifetime. We knew that tomorrow was not guaranteed. Reflecting on some of the dynamic cities that we visited during our first three-month trip together, we decided to take short trips back to those locations. We desired to revisit Washington (DC), Boston, Chicago, New Orleans, and San Francisco. We also wanted to share these experiences with Brenda, Robert, and family members.

The first major trip would take us to Europe. At the time, Sandye's Hilton Head friend, Dianne, lived in London, with her husband Larry. We started making plans to fly to Paris and then visit Larry and Dianne in London. We told them we were coming a few months before but had not set a date. Now that I was traveling all over for work accruing points with the airlines, I wanted to spoil Sandye and take her on first class, which also would alleviate extra stress and discomfort. I was able to push her down the Jetway in the wheelchair and up to the plane's door. With help, Sandye would struggle to pull herself up, hold onto the doorways and grab each seat while navigating to her seat.

I did not know what tomorrow would bring so I acted on a spur of the moment impulse once the trip began. Her walker and wheelchair were loaded along with our luggage. First class was a big deal and very luxurious. We consumed steak and seafood, hot fudge sundaes, followed with hot towels, complimentary cocktails, and movies. I knew that it would be next to impossible to take Sandye on another trip in coach class. We had set a precedent, and I would have to save up a lot of Airline miles for future trips. Landing in Paris began with some obstacles. Wheelchair signs were displayed everywhere we looked, but without any instructions or directives. The sidewalks were old, with most of them being made of cobblestones. I had learned back in the States, when the terrain was bumpy, to tip Sandye back so her feet were up in the air. It made it easier to get past rough areas that a person in a wheelchair would not be able to pass through by themselves. It is harder on Sandye but she treated it like being on a ride and worked through it. It started to make sense that we had not seen anyone in a wheelchair throughout the city. Menus were hard to read, and very little English was spoken. Still, we were going to make sure that we soaked in every moment.

The first stop on our bucket list was the Louvre Museum. We had learned of its many works of art, sculptures and other masterpieces on display and couldn't wait to see them. Handicapped people were treated differently. On arrival, I moved Sandye to an entry door and we were pleasantly surprised that no one collected a fee. We thought, at first, that it was a holiday, and everyone was not charged. After entering, our eyes marveled at a huge quilt of the Last Supper. It was the size of a house. We took pictures and then passed other great works of art, including the painting of the "Mona Lisa" and the statue of the famous "Venus De Milo." As we entered a ballroom called "Statuary," which was the size of a stadium, we stopped in our tracks. Our eyes slowly scanned this unbelievable site. Our jaws dropped to the floor. There were hundreds of full body statues on three levels. From where we viewed, you could see all the statues until they were too many, disappearing to the back of the room. We learned that one statue could have taken a lifetime for one artist to complete. A person would not have to love art to be blown away by that view. We wanted to freeze this spectacular moment in our minds to remember it forever. We had left the Louvre joyously knowing that we had seen things that were one of a kind in the world. As I was pushing her around the city, we could see across the Seine River to our left a beautiful site in the distance.

Sandye: "Look, Kent, it is the Eiffel Tower," with excitement in her voice. "Let's go right over there."

As we started to cross the bridge over the river, we noticed the beautiful Notre Dame Cathedral on our right. We brought some throw away cameras, knowing we needed to capture every moment in its purist form. Cell phones were not invented yet. As we neared the Eiffel tower, we could feel the magnificence of this majestic structure. I helped Sandye move over to a park bench and tucked the wheelchair out of site. Sandye always made the point that MS does not define her, and she expected people to treat her the same as everyone else. As we sat cuddling on the park bench basking in the moment, a popping noise rang out in the air.

Sandye: "What was that?"

Kent: "I have no idea."

Then another noise, POP, POP, POP, right in front of us as we realized all the lights were illuminating on the tower. We were screaming with joy, as we were being treated to the magical surprise only God could have gifted us. The whole tower was now lit up for all the city of Paris to see. We felt like it was our own private event that no one could take from our memory. Love was in the air. We cuddled and kissed, relishing in the moment. We purchased numerous replicas of the tower that reside in our home as a reminder.

One phrase that I knew was, "Carpe Diem," or seize the day. That captured the moment. Whether she had MS or not, our motto was to live every moment going full tilt. Tomorrow is not promised for any of us.

Next, we wanted to see the Palace of Versailles. First, we tried to take a city bus. When the bus pulled up, I was happy to see a wheelchair sign on the side of it. When the door opened the driver signaled to me that our chair had no access. This was confusing, but not to be deterred, we decided to take the train/subway. I wheeled her to the subway only to find out that there were no elevators. The city was kept as original as possible without the modern conveniences. The only way to board meant going down a hundred and fifty steps, but there were handicap signs at the top of the stairs. No wonder that we did not see anyone else in a wheelchair. We were going to that Palace over my dead body, so we had to figure it out. I knew how to position the wheelchair to handle the steps one at a time, by tilting her back and going straight down. But there still was a loud thump sound (blam, blam, blam). Sandye did not want to miss going, so she was up to the task. Two men saw me and quickly came to help lift the chair with Sandye down the last fifty steps. God bless them.

Once we reached the bottom, a man dressed in an orange vest saw us coming and began hollering in French to people in a back room. Four men came hurrying out when the subway arrived. As the train pulled up and the doors flung open, the men knew they only had a couple seconds to react. They placed two boards that bridged the gap from the pavement to the inside of the train. Then they guided Sandye's wheelchair onto the boards and maneuvered her onto the train. If they had not been there, there would have been no way to board the train. Sandye thanked them all and made it a fun moment. As the train was making stops, we realized we might have missed our stop. I asked if anyone spoke English. One nice gentleman spoke enough to help us. He said that we had to go back one stop and that he would help us. So, as the train pulled up, an employee saw that we wanted to get off. He rang a bell. Four men came running out to do their duty and help Sandye off the train.

Sandye: "Here come my friends to save the day." (with a big smile on her face)

The gentleman helping us chose to get off the train and go back the other direction. He changed his plans to make sure that we found our way safely. We thanked him for being so kind and tried to pay him for his kindness. He would not have it. We were shocked and moved by his compassion. Contrary to what we had heard prior to the trip, the people in France were very kind to us everywhere we went.

We were off to the palace which was about three blocks away. I really had to tip Sandye well back in the chair and carefully maneuvered the cobblestone path. We heard the thump, thump, boom, boom sound of the wheelchair as we headed toward the palace. There was a long line of visitors waiting to enter. We were waiting our turn at the end of the line in an open-air plaza outside. An employee made her way to the back of the line and motioned for us to come with her.

Sandye: "Why does she want us to get out of the line?"

Kent: "I'm not sure. Maybe they saw us on a video and wanted to help us like on the subway."

So, a bit confused, we followed her past the long line of everyone waiting. She took us in a special door and saved us about a half an hour waiting in that line. We really had no idea why we got special privileges but enjoyed it. Once we got inside the palace, no one charged us any fees to be there. We were beginning to realize that the rules for handicapped people were different than in the United States. It was harder to get around and not easy or handicapped accessible, but everyone would go out of their way to help us. That left us with a great feeling. A quirky gentleman, who was an employee of the palace, aggressively motioned to me that he was going to step in and push Sandye a different direction through a door. He pointed for me to go down a flight of stairs. Behind Sandye's back, he pointed to a place on a map where I was to meet him. I was taken back a little having to let him drive her but assumed they would be okay, because we were in a public place. She had no idea what was happening. He looked like he was having fun pushing her as she hurried off down a hallway. Sandye really did not know what was going on. All of a sudden, she realized that he had taken her away from me. Sandye started addressing the man with fear in her voice as they went away.

Sandye: "Sir! Sir!"

The man smiled at me as he took her away, and I knew that I would see her in just a minute down a flight of stairs. I assumed they would take an elevator to get there.

Unbeknownst to me, Sandye was scared that this man could have taken her anywhere and harmed her. As they came out of the elevator, I was shocked to see fear in her face that I had not seen before.

Sandye: "Don't you ever do that again." (with a shaken furious tone)

Kent: "Do what?"

Sandye: "Leave me alone with a stranger. I was scared to death."

I never wanted to put her in that situation again. I now realized that when someone gives up their freedom and control of their own situation in a wheelchair, they are at your mercy to help them. I cannot underestimate that importance. I thought the man was kind of funny and let her go with him. I did not realize that she was afraid. That was a big lesson and would not happen again. From that point on, I would protect her in every situation. After Sandye settled down, we proceeded to a ballroom floor, which was built by King Louis in 1631. It was the infamous "Hall of mirrors." This spectacular room had two-hundred-forty feet of mirrors on one side. On the opposite wall were beautiful windows facing out to a courtyard of fountains. There were beautiful Fresco paintings on the ceiling. You could only imagine the magnificent parties that were thrown in this room back in the 1600's. We knew we would never see anything like this unimaginable space again. There was nothing in the world like what we were viewing at this moment. Sandye, forgetting the drama earlier, lost herself in a beautiful moment dreaming of the silk ball gowns the women of the time must have worn.

Sandye: "Can you imagine the classy events and parties we
would have been at, if we were here in the 1600's."

After cherishing this unimaginable palace, we had a nice lunch in an
open-air patio restaurant and then found our way back to the hotel dreaming of what was to come next.

We went to shop in the local grocery store a couple times. The ceiling was
low, and I hate to say it, but the whole room smelled like body odor. Many
people did not wear deodorant and did not care about spending that kind
of money on perfume. We wanted to hurry in and out of there. Sandye
was always very smell oriented and covered her nose the whole time. While
waiting in a long line to check out, everyone began to point for us to pass
them in line and go to the front.

Sandye: "Why do they keep doing this, making us cut in the
line? They were here first."

This was the second day in a row in this store when they did this. Once,
passing all of the people feeling uncomfortable at the front of the line I
asked:

Kent: "Does anybody speak English?"

One lady who spoke broken English said, "I do. What do you need?"

Kent: "I have a question for you. We do not want to be rude
and move to the front of the line. Why does everyone keep
insisting that we go in front of them?"

Lady: "In the stores we have a special line for the handicapped people to use. If no one is handicapped, everyone else will use it. When you arrived, this is your line and your line only. It is our country's rule."

Sandye: "I am humbled by this respect. Can you please call our country and tell them to do this?"

We laughed and smiled, knowing that there are many things each country could adopt from another to help people.

The next day we wandered through the city coming to the very famous "Champs-Elysees". It was a street over a mile long with outdoor cafes and seating as far you could see. There were fresh Gellato shops everywhere. People from all over the world were relaxing on patios without a care as far as you could see. The environment was festive, whimsical, and felt like a dream. We enjoyed a lunch on a patio.

Sandye: "This is perfect. The only thing I would change is that I would love for my best friend Brenda to be able to share this joy with us."

I was determined, that on future trips, we would figure out how to get Brenda and Robert to go with us. After we finished our meal, we headed to the end of the plaza to see one of the most famous tourist attractions in the world, "The Arc de Triomphe". I remembered this place from a movie. Chevy Chase was driving in a circle around the Arc going so fast that he could without exiting the road. It was a very funny scene but when seeing the crazy traffic it made sense.

Sandye: "Let's get a picture with the Arc de Triomphe in the background."

Knowing this would be kind of dangerous, I was always up for living on the edge. We gave our camera to another tourist and I helped her out of her wheelchair holding her tight. We carefully maneuvered down this very narrow peninsula with traffic now whisking by in both directions.

Kent: "Sandye don't let go of me and hurry up. (smiling)"

In median at Arc de Triomphe

She laughed, enjoying the challenge while feeling the car's wind a couple feet from us on both sides with the Arc de Triomphe right behind us. With his eyes not believing that we were doing this, the man took the picture, knowing that if we fell off balance either way we would be struck by a car. With adrenaline rushing through our veins from excitement, we eased back the wheelchair. The world would not take Sandye's freedom today. MS would not define her. As we came down from our high, we decided it was too difficult to get across that street to climb the "Arc" and we had seen enough. We started to look for a taxi to go a few miles back to the hotel. There was a line of about a hundred people waiting for taxis. As we waited, there was a commotion up at the front of the line. A gentleman was falling as he was getting into a taxi, while everyone in the line was watching him. He either was disabled or probably drank too much. As we watched helplessly, the man fell onto the ground. The fifty people in line in front of us just stared at him.

Sandye: "Kent, go help that man right now. He needs help. Go to him. Hurry."

Never doubting her word, I ran past all of the people and helped the man off of the floor and into the taxi. The driver and all the people just watched as I helped the obviously incapacitated inebriated man first onto the floor of the taxi and then up onto the seat. Even in his state you could see he was so thankful that someone helped him.

Sandye: "Thank you. We always have to help those in need."

Every instinct that Sandye learned from her mother and father as a child was to act immediately and do the right thing. I knew she was right, but also knew I would have to change my thoughts going forward. I would now be the one to act when needed and not be the one standing by watching helplessly like I would have done in the past. We didn't have to settle for who I was before. I could choose to change my character. Thank you, my dear love Sandye for showing me this lesson.

Paris is full of memories and lessons that I hold in my heart forever! I also learned that the people in Paris were not mean like I had heard they might be. They were structured, proud, and expected people to respect their culture. Special orders do upset them, as they are not a fast food nation. The menu is firm and changes are not permitted in their country. When we understood this, and did not try to change their ways, we saw a beautiful country with people who truly cared for our well-being. The people of Paris did not charge us anything in all public places. I could not believe the amount of money that we saved. We were very humbled by that and greatly appreciative.

The next phase of our trip would take us to see Dianne and Larry in London. A railroad, that travelled under the English Channel called "The Chunnell" whisked us from Paris to London. We went first class. The ladies serving us were very formally dressed and served us a first-class meal. I was learning that spending the extra dollar was worth every new memory captured. Sandye loved Dianne and learned to love Larry as well, although we really did not get to see him. He was always off working. His character was that of a financially practical businessman. I was as different from Larry at this time as two people could be. We laughed about him being a bit stuffy and we just focused on Dianne. As we got to know him we became close. Now, Larry was well respected and loved. President George Bush elevated him to the position of Secretary of the Department of Education. He won many prestigious awards. At this time, he was a senior partner for the company Deloitte and Touché, featured as one of five top managers in their annual business magazine covering all of Europe. I thought of him as a successful man and a very good friend.

Everywhere we went we received royal treatment. After reaching London, my "from the hip" nature bit me. We were now at the train station in London. I suddenly realized, we did not have Larry and Dianne's address or phone number. I tried to get the operator's assistance to reach them.

> Sandye: "How could you come all the way across the world and not have their contact information with you?"

In the past, as my mother would always do, I thought of five different ways to fix the problem I had created (except she would do it at any cost, not concerned if it was hurting anyone else). The operator could not give us the number but agreed to call them with my message that included a call back number.

> Larry: (Astonished that we called them out of the blue) "We didn't know when you were coming."

> Kent: "That's my fault. I am too impetuous."

> Larry: "Well we are excited that you are here. We will work it out. Have the taxi bring you to the address I am going to give you."

As we went to get in the taxi, there was no one helping us like they did in France. I had to take several trips back and forth, putting the luggage into the cab while the driver sat and watched. Sandye, knowing it was going to be different...

> Sandye: "I want to go back to France where they catered to
> my every need and did not charge me for it."

We belly laughed at that one.

Larry and Dianne's flat, that his company furnished, was on the sixth floor and it was majestic. The man at the front gate called up to their home and then let us in. He helped get all our suitcases and handicapped equipment up to their classy two-bedroom apartment, which overlooked a gorgeous view of the Queen's castle. Sandye could not take her eyes off the magnificent horses.

> Dianne: "Look Sandye, across the street. That big building is
> the Castle where Princess Diana currently lives."

That is all it took. The fairytale trip continued. Sandye stayed permanently in clouds of joy. She woke up each morning and would hear the Queen's horses coming out of the Castle and down the street.

> Sandye: "Hurry Kent. Let's get ready. The Queen is ready to
> see us."

She would get her walker and sing, as she struggled across the apartment to catch a glimpse of the beautiful horses parading up and down the street. She was having the time of her life, creating "Joy through the Journey." I was right with her every step, loving her that much more. She couldn't wait. Larry had to go to another country for a couple of days while Dianne showed us around London. We went out for a very nice lunch and made sure that we purchased them a gift card from the restaurant. I was learning to make sure we thanked everyone appropriately for treating us.

Dianne took us to Buckingham Palace just before the changing of the guard. There were hundreds, if not thousands, of tourists there. We were allowed to move all the way up to the front gate, because of the wheelchair, so Sandye could be safe and see everything. We would have loved to be standing without the wheelchair but would graciously accept the opportunity to have the best view ever! The changing of the guard was majestic and over the top. The horses and guards were dressed perfectly and did not miss a step. They came within a few feet of us as we were right by the entrance. Then, just as we thought the event was over, a hush came over the crowd. Then a frenzy of excitement filled the air. People started screaming with joy. A convoy of vehicles was coming towards the castle.

Dianne: "Oh my goodness Sandye, look. What a great surprise. It's the Queen coming back to the castle."

As the crowd roared and cheered, the Queen was waving.

Sandye: "Look she is waving. I think she is was waving at me." (laughing)

We loved it. God seems to put us in the perfect spot if we will just let him. The next morning came and Larry was back from his trip. Off we went. We had to take a bus to the outskirts of England to Berkshire, where the Windsor Castle is located. It is the queen's second home and the largest castle in all of London. While she is not living there, people are allowed to tour the castle. We needed to take a bus out to the castle. Getting Sandye on and off the high steps on the bus was tricky. It was not handicap accessible. I got in front of her, grabbed under her arms, and struggled helping her lift each leg up the high steps to board. People tried to help, but there was not enough room. It was too awkward and inconvenient to help push her from the back, so we made do.

Sandye: "Kent, I am not going to miss this castle, so do whatever you have to do to get me on and off this bus."

When we arrived at the castle everyone got off the bus first, including Larry and Dianne. I looked at the steep steps and knew this was going to be dangerous for her to go down.

Sandye: "How are we going to do this?"

Kent: "Hold on. I've got you."

The only way I could get her off the bus was to lift and carry her".

Kent: "Throw your arms around my neck and do not let go for anything."

With a little hesitancy, she latched onto my neck. I powered through, picked her up, and squeezed down the aisle. Carefully and slowly, I took huge steps down, wobbling to each side. The last step was the biggest to get off the bus. Larry watched intently, as I finally got her to a resting place in the wheelchair. In that instance Larry began to change the way he treated and respected me. I was just doing what I had to do for my bride.

We went into the castle and viewed royal bedrooms. The tour guide said it was time to go upstairs to view this huge dollhouse that was especially made for the princess by the queen. The tour guide said it was time to go upstairs and view the royal bedrooms. He came to Sandye, seeing her joy in this whole situation and said:

Tour guide: "And you, young lady. Do you want to have royal treatment and ride in style in the Queen Mother's elevator? We do not usually open this up, but something was telling me you needed special treatment. They had made a special small elevator just for the Queen Mother. It would barely fit one person and our wheelchair."

Sandye: "Why of course sir, I would be honored, and I have got to see this dollhouse."

I just shook my head in awe of the experiences that we were having. Sandye would put herself out there and was rewarded at every turn. It was like a fairytale ending to the trip, and our relationship with Larry went deeper. Dianne was always a close friend of ours. Her laugh and joy rings in our ears every time we think of her. We couldn't thank them enough for this grand experience.

When the trip was over and we arrived home, I loaded the pictures for Sandye to view on the TV. We laughed together and enjoyed reliving the moments. Years later, Dianne passed away from cancer. It was a sad day in our life. Larry has stayed in touch ever since, calling every three months. He doesn't miss a call. He told me that he only reaches out to two people, an older man and myself.

Kent: "What did you think about me when you first met me waiting tables on Hilton Head with Sandye?"

Larry: "From a business perspective, I thought you were a loser."

This comment hurt for me to hear.

Larry: "Kent, I have hired and judged thousands of people over the years at my company and I am never wrong about my gut instinct. That is what I was paid to do. But with you I was wrong. I watched you over the years go from a wild, unruly, fun, happy-go-lucky person to getting a degree and a good job. My respect completely changed for you when you married Sandye years after you knew that she had a progressive disease. You owned that situation and still do. When I saw you handle her on that bus in London, I knew that I was wrong and had misjudged you. I am staying in touch with you because I am watching you do things that very few men would ever do. I have not seen this kind of love personally before."

These comments stopped me in my tracks, especially from a man that had been so steady and successful throughout his career. Larry didn't respect many people, but I earned a very high measure as he watched me care for Sandye. Larry's first impression of me was one of a fun-loving man who lacked character. Now he sees me as a committed husband and caretaker. Love changed me, God's love and my love for Sandye.

***

Chip, chip, chip. The artist's work seemed to show compassion. Slowly, my personality started to change. My compulsive behavior needed a heart transplant that showed love, compassion, and genuine concern for those who enter my world. I knew that I had to see and react quickly to needs that come up. Not only was I learning to respect others, but I was gaining respect in the process.

Gambling Piece Chiseled

All was going well with my work and I was attending gambling anonymous meetings. It was not as bad as Hilton Head, but I still had my moments. Sandye kept her eyes and ears open for opportunities to learn more about God. She was having devotionals with a friend down the street, when they learned that Joyce Meyer was coming to the Phillips Arena in downtown Atlanta. Sandye enjoyed listening to her speak on TV. While I was working, they attended the Friday morning session at the conference. That night, Sandye returned excited about the experience. She shared that another session was scheduled the next morning and wanted me to join her. I was game. I never experienced a Christian conference.

So off we went. I was wearing casual shorts and a t-shirt, not wanting to stand out. We sat in the balcony's second deck. There were thousands of people there. It was very exciting with upbeat worship music. The complex was filled with amazing diversity. Joyce Meyer was preaching for TV and had a great connection with the audience. Then the TV cameras were turned off. Joyce began sharing more private topics like the Holy Spirit. This was all new to me, but I was intrigued.

Then she began speaking about bad habits and how to break them with Jesus' help. After throwing cigarettes onto the stage, she made the call for everyone who desired to stop smoking to come forward. I watched as hundreds or even thousands of people flocked the stage. Joyce prayed over them. I could not know how her prayers were answered but felt something new, nevertheless. Then God moved in that place in a big way. After everyone was dispersed, Joyce paused.

> Joyce: "I was going to do this next session tonight, but the Holy Spirit just told me to do it now. Anyone who has a gambling problem needs to come down here right now."

I sat back in my seat and could not believe what I was hearing. I Looked straight at Sandye.

> Kent: "Did you know they were going to cover this?"

> Sandye: "They don't have a program in these conferences."

I felt very uncomfortable.

> Joyce: "Come on now. Everyone with this problem need to come down right now."

Eight people came forward, unlike the hundreds with the cigarette addiction.

> Kent: "I can't go down there. Many people from Coca-Cola are probably here. That would be very embarrassing."

Sandye was silent as if praying to herself. At this point it looked like Joyce was not happy with the amount of people.

Joyce: "I want you in the second deck to come down right now."

She pointed right at me (I couldn't believe what was happening at that moment). I squirmed, got mad and screamed "All right." I got up, worked my way out of the balcony, and made my way down through an entrance onto the main floor. I was the thirteenth person to reach the stage. Joyce then prayed over the gambling addiction. The crowd raised their hands and was very vocal. I could feel a heavy presence, not knowing what it was. She prayed hard for all of us to be free of this problem. Then she came down off the stage and started at the far end of the line. When she got to me she said, "In the name of Jesus, be healed," while hitting my forehead with the palm of her hand. The next thing I knew, I was lying flat on my back. The whole crowd was praising God. All thirteen people had fallen like a bowling ball striking the pins.

Joyce went back up on the stage. Her assistants helped me off the floor. I had a disbelief feeling. I knew a strong power came over me that would trigger a strong change in my life. When I got back up to Sandye, I noticed that she had been crying. I sat back down in a daze, unsure of what just happened. My compulsion did not disappear overnight. It diminished slowly as other things began to replace the habit. Sandye's message was for me to focus on positive things. Gambling was certainly not one of those, but that seminar had a significant impact on me. Sandye's tears were not from sadness.

***

Chip, chip, chip. The work began to have eyes appear like they penetrated the viewers. Joyce was looking directly into my eyes from a long distance away, like a laser beam and it caused me to jump. I knew that was going to be a turning point from the hold that gambling had on me, and it started the healing process. I also knew that the Holy Spirit would be there to assist me in the journey.

New Career Path

After three years of working at Coca-Cola, Rudy became my boss. He was one of the first senior black executives at the company. We travelled throughout the southeast, calling on colleges and universities. He shared many stories of racism that he experienced over the years. In one discussion, I was telling Rudy:

Kent: "I am really impressed with your boss, the vice-president and want to be like him." (I had to have what others had like my mother)

Rudy: "What are you doing? He can't create customer relationships like you, so don't put other people on pedestals."

That shook me to my core, and I started having more confidence in everything I would do in business. I won a sales award and now, I felt like I finally made it in the business world where I belong. Coca-Cola scheduled a meeting in Houston. At the same time, I was offered a regional sales manager position at a smaller juice company. This was a bigger job in a smaller company. I loved the Coca-Cola brand but was frustrated watching lifetime employees lose their jobs. The industry was changing, and people were not staying with one company for their entire careers. Rudy, my new boss, wanted me to stay and told me that I was about to win another award. I was told to board a plane and make the meeting. I made a lifechanging decision to leave Coca-Cola at the time, taking a position as a regional sales manager for a juice company. So, I made the decision to stay home and leave Coca-Cola for the smaller company. This company sold small juice cups supplied for school systems.

That job took me travelling out of state. I thrived in this sales environment and my numbers were going through the roof. I learned a lot of business practices at Coca-Cola. My new position involved teaching other salespeople the things I learned. The VP, named Bob Gats, came to me.

> Bob: "Go train the other salespeople to do what you do to get the results that you get. Also, call on other corporate accounts like airlines, cruise lines, stadiums, and caterers."

This solidified a solid relationship with Bob.

I was now covering eight states as a regional sales manager. I have used all of the training tools I learned at Coca-Cola there ever since.

Joyce Landau Story

Most of us have had positive experiences with nurse care givers. When our health is compromised, we tend to think that they have our best interests at heart. The term, "nursing home," takes on a very different perspective. Although, many of these places may offer quality services for their guests, that was not the case for Joyce Landau, who suffered from multiple sclerosis (MS).

Dr. Stuart suggested to Sandye that she should attend a support group for people with MS. She found a group in Snellville, about forty minutes south. We went together to her first meeting. We sat in a circle with about fifteen others. Just as the meeting was about to start, the door opened and the paramedic was pushing a lady who was very debilitated, while a friend walked behind her. The leader of the group asked if the new people would identify themselves and where they are from.

> Sandye: "My name is Sandye, and this is my husband, Kent. We live about a half an hour away."

The lady in the wheelchair was not speaking. Her head was down.

> Lady's friend: "My name is Nancy. This is my friend Joyce. She has trouble speaking, so, we are just going to watch."

The meeting continued, where many people would talk about the struggles that they had with MS. Sandye was not comfortable in this environment. She knew that it helped some people, but she did not want to focus on the tough parts of MS. She desired to continually look forward. She opposed many of the comments made by the other participants and was not ready to talk about those topics. That was the last time we went to a support group like that. When the meeting was over, Sandye hurried directly over to Joyce. Most people shunned Joyce because of her degree of disability but Sandye wouldn't have it.

> Sandye: "Hi. It's nice to meet you."

She reached out and grabbed Joyce's withered hand as she looked directly into her eyes. A smile came to Joyce's face and a small response.

Joyce: "Hello."

I asked Joyce's friend where Joyce lived. She told me that a medical transport had brought her from a local nursing home.

Sandye: "Joyce, would you mind if we come to see you?"

Joyce: (barely able to speak said softly) "That would be nice."

You could see the light in her eyes though her body was weak and frail. Sandye was determined to go see her as soon as possible. As soon as we entered the nursing home, Sandye said:

Sandye: "This place smells to high heaven."

On the first visit we saw three beds in Joyce's room. She was closest to the window. Her body was in a fetal position. It was obvious that she had not had physical therapy in a while. Sandye went up to the bed and grabbed Joyce's hand.

Sandye: "Hi, Joyce. It's so good to see you again."

As Joyce reached out, she grimaced in pain. Every movement she made was painful. Her speech was more like a whisper. We were not sure if it was MS or from not enough fluids. Sandye noticed the photos on the dresser with Joyce's family.

Sandye: "Joyce. I see that you like to travel and have a beautiful family."

You could now see the joy in her face as her eyes lit up. Here was a person with an amazing past, revealed through her pictures and she was now reduced to a painful, crumpled up body. After speaking with her for a little while, Sandye realized that Joyce's only joy was watching the TV to her left.

Joyce: (whispering) "I only get three channels."

Sandye: "Well, we have to see about that."

On the way home, Sandye shared about what we had just witnessed.

Sandye: "I need to call Pastor Steve."

Kent: "Pastor Steve?"

Sandye: "He needs to come with me to that place. It's disgusting."

Kent: "What can he do?"

Sandye: "I don't know, but something must be done!"

I decided to take pastor Steve to see Joyce. I gave him advanced warning of what to expect. When we walked up to her bed, Steve put his hand on hers. A small glow came to her face, knowing that two men were giving her attention. I mentioned to Joyce that I knew she loved animals. We brought a beautiful poster of a tiger. She could see the ceiling and TV from her bed. We pinned the poster to the ceiling above her head. Pastor Steve prayed with her. As we left the nursing home, Pastor Steve became furious.

> Steve: "I can't believe this. People come to me every day with all kinds of complaints. Then you look at the state that this once beautiful lady is in. (Raising his voice even louder) These are the people we should be helping. This is where I should be spending my time."

He was both mad and ashamed at the same time.

The next six months became a mission for Sandye. Every day she called the cable company and the nursing home to get Joyce more channels. At first, half the nursing home had cable. The rest did not. We kept constant communication with Joyce's friend and she told us that Joyce's husband could not handle the MS and left. Two sisters, living close by, were not visiting her. Finally, after a long battle Joyce got her cable TV. Joyce could not move without feeling the pain. The word, "ooh" prefaced every word that she spoke. She was happy that Sandye fought for her. You could feel the love between the two. About a year later, I received a call from Joyce's friend that she had passed away. I was mowing the lawn and saw Sandye through the window. I shut the mower off and ran inside.

> Kent: "Sandye. Please sit down."

> Sandye: "What's wrong?"

Kent: "I just received a call that Joyce Landau has passed away."

We immediately broke into tears.

Kent: "Sandy. I will protect you. I will never let that happen to you, over my dead body."

***

Sandye was experiencing severe abdominal pain. We went to a specialist. After performing several tests, surgery was the next option. Previous surgeries left a large scar, where the doctors needed to open once again. The doctor was overwhelmed by the excess scarring tissue from the previous surgeries. He could not identify the organs properly. Not wanting to harm her, he backed out of the surgery. That caused more pain without resolution. We decided to deal with the pain without surgery or explanation until it finally subsided.

One Sunday church visit after Pastor Steve talked about the war in Bosnia, a family from there was in attendance. They fled from Bosnia with nothing to their name. He asked if anyone could help the family. It would be greatly appreciated. When we came home, Sandye sat at the kitchen table and felt led to help them. We called the church and asked the family to come to visit so that we could give them her car. Sandye said it was time for a new one, anyway. She asked the man for one dollar. Happily, and in tears, he drove away with his family. They did not speak English but their faces provided all the thanks needed. These acts of compassion from Sandye were slowly changing me forever. I cannot express the deep feeling of contentment that I had when watching the complete joy and relief on all the family's faces during this life changing experience.

We decided to spend birthdays and holidays with our neighbors Russ and Leslie. We had common interests. We planned to go to their house on Sandye's birthday. They were making seafood platters and we were bringing appetizers. Their house was across the street but well down a steep hill. Sandye would have to hold on to my arm and the walk would be too difficult with her fading abilities. We put everything in the car. I could see that she was struggling physically trying to get into the car. We drove down to their garage. They had a walk up stairs to get to the main level of the house.

Sandye: "I don't think I can get up the stairs."

Kent: "Let me see what I can do."

I ran up the stairs to the back door to speak to Russ and Leslie.

Russ: "Well, we still want to have fun with you. If she can't come to us, we'll bring the party to her."

It was cold out and I pulled the car into the garage. Russ told me to keep the garage door open and the car running. We brought all the platters and beverages into the car. The CD played our favorite music. We had fun just as we would have inside their house. After an hour and a half, their children poked their heads out into the garage with confused looks. Russ rolled down the window.

> Russ: "This is an adult only party. You're not invited. Go find something to do."

He slapped me with a high five. Then we resumed partying for three hours, eating shrimp cocktails and having the time of our life. We were not going to let Sandye's disability diminish our joy.

***

Chip, chip, chip. Compassion enters in a big way. The act of giving from the heart reaps rewards. Respect is earned and not something to be viewed on a pedestal. Acts of love add to the final appeal that the artist desires.

Millenium

With the new millennium coming, we wanted to do something special with Brenda and Robert. We travelled to Chicago, where Sandye and I previously visited, to welcome in the new year. We stayed at the Hyatt Hotel on the river near the Miracle Mile, which is the heart of the city. This hotel had a five-story high window view from the bar. You could see Lake Michigan. We were on top of the world. Our Hilton Head friend Jared brought a date and joined us. We went to a high-end steak restaurant, where the Tampa Bay Buccaneer football players were dining. Robert and I wore white tuxedoes. The girls were dressed to "the nine." On our way back to the hotel before midnight we heard a commotion on the street. To our amazement, we saw a man dressed as Jesus dragging a huge cross on his shoulders down the middle of the street. Brenda and Robert laughed it off, but I pondered what that meant in my heart. At the hotel we partied at the bar for New Years Eve. A man came up to us in an Elvis costume.

> Robert: "Our night is fulfilled. We saw Jesus and Elvis in the same night."

We all laughed. We vowed to have many more trips and experiences with Brenda and Robert.

In the previous year we bought season tickets to the Atlanta Falcon football games. Sandye was not into the sport but wanted to do things with me that I enjoyed. On the flip side, I agreed to start enjoying shopping (which I hated but learned to enjoy over years of practice). Our seats at the stadium supported handicapped people. Sandye was happy, that the wheelchair could be hidden while she moved to her seat like everyone else. She loved to cheer, even though she didn't understand the game. We enjoyed ourselves with the other season ticket holders. Then there was a play on the field where the opposing player rushed through the line prematurely and threw our quarterback on the ground. The crowd screamed and booed at the player. Then it quieted down. In breaking the complete silence, Sandye screamed at the top of her lungs:

Sandye: "Hey big boy, Take your hands off our man. Don't make me come down there."

Another girl yelled: "That a girl, Sandye. You tell them."

Kent: "Sandye, SHHH!"

Sandye: "I paid for my ticket. I can say whatever I want and you don't shush me."

I gave up and we laughed. It was so much fun. The dead silence turned into hilarious laughter all around. Having these season tickets was a benefit, in that we could acquire Super Bowl tickets there the following year. We entered the lottery and won two tickets for the event. In exchange for a shopping spree, Sandye gave up her ticket. That allowed me to take my boss. We went to the game during an ice storm and the game came down to the last play. It was exhilarating. I started to see the blessings that God was allowing me to enjoy. Afterwards, I patiently went shopping with Sandye and watched her pick out the items of her dreams.

Sandye was concealing her MS symptoms to the public and my family. I am not sure why, except that she did not want to be a liability. Around this time she was having horrible migraines. Nothing seemed to give her relief. One time the pain was so bad on the weekend, that I was desperate and searched for Dr. Stuart's home number. I reached his machine and left a message. He called back with instructions.

> Dr Stuart: "Put a bandana around her head and tie it as tight as you can."

This provided some relief but it was a hard journey. At the time, we were using a chiropractor and neurologist for advice. Her symptoms needed various medical professionals to assist in her care at this time. MS can be debilitating for both the patient and the caregivers. Everyone who has the disease experiences symptoms differently. It is very hard to predict what happens next. I have learned coping skills through the consult of many medical and psychological professionals. I sincerely hope that others, going through similar situations, will seek the help they need.

We needed a bigger house to hold an office or add a second story to our existing house. Moving away from Russ and Leslie weighed heavy. We found a compromise fifteen minutes away in the same town. This allowed us to continue our holiday traditions shooting fireworks, partying and enjoying fellowship. Sandye started using a walker. She was still able to drive while putting the walker in the back seat and balancing herself to get into the front seat.

Humor Break

Sandye was starting new medicines that were extra strength and contained steroids. We did not know how she was going to react or deal with the side effects. She was having difficulty falling asleep at night, probably due to the steroids, so she took a double strength sedative for the first time. She was using her walker while I was standing on the side of the kitchen island. She was sitting on her walker seat while boiling some noodles on one burner and cooking two vegetables on the others. As I was talking, her body started to go limp. She slowly began slipping towards the floor.

Kent: "Sandye, you're slipping. You're going to fall."

Sandye: "Really. Wow!" (never taking her eyes off the stove)

Before I could get to her, she started to fall. I lunged and caught her before she hit the floor. Then I eased her down. Her body was like a wet noodle as I slowly laid her head on the kitchen floor. She was focused on the boiling noodles and vegetables. Sternly, she began giving instructions.

Sandye: "Don't let those noodles boil too much and check the beans."

Now what was I to do? She was laid out on the floor. There was a recliner in the living room that backs up to the kitchen. Knowing she could not get back up to sit on the walker, Sandye told me to drag her over to the recliner, so she could keep her eye on the food as a great Italian cook would do. So, I proceeded to put my hands under her arms like firemen do and dragged her through the kitchen in front of the floor to ceiling windows with full view of at least two neighbors watching from their adjoining yards. The thought of the movie, "Rear Window," with Jimmy Stuart immediately came to my mind. In that movie Jimmy Stuart watched Raymond Burr kill his wife and then drag her through the house in front of the windows. Sandye was now laying comfortably but to the neighbors she may have appeared lifeless or dead. As I was dragging her, Sandye never missed a beat.

Sandye: "Check the noodles again."

Now it looks like dinner might burn. She was dead weight, and I wasn't letting go. Once I reached the recliner, I used some caregiver techniques to leverage and lift her up to the chair. Never taking her eyes off the stove she responded:

Sandy: "Push my back down."

So, I did, and she laid horizontally. Now her body was in the living room. The head of the recliner stretched into the kitchen so she could see everything. She was still giving stern instructions:

Sandye: "Did you put a noodle under the water to taste it?"

Before she could get another word out, the sedative kicked in and she let out a huge snore mid-sentence:

Sandye: "Watch out for the ZZZ." (fades into unconsciousness)

Kent: (mumbling to himself) "Dear God. Please don't let the neighbors phone the police after seeing me dragging Sandye's snoring body by all of the patio windows."

Knowing I had no idea as to what to cook next, I turned off all the burners. Then I went for a blanket and covered her. She proceeded to sleep sixteen hours in that chair and woke up well rested. I slept beside her on the couch.

Luckily, when the neighbors conveniently stopped by the next couple of days, Sandye was alive and well. I always refer to that story as the "Rear Window" story. (Thank you Jimmy Stewart for the memories) I am not sure if Sandye remembers it.

***

Chip, chip, chip. The sculpture takes on multiple facets as one does not appear alone. The importance of fellowship and prayer is introduced in a big way. We do not need to face our trials alone. Our walk of faith with prayer and fellowship go deeper. Moments of humor are great stress relievers.

9-11

I had been calling on large national accounts. This particular week, I was in Chicago, ready to make a sales call to sell juice cups to American Airlines. I was getting ready in the hotel across the street from their office, when I heard a special alert on the TV. A plane had hit the first tower in New York. My appointment was in forty-five minutes. I continued to get ready while watching in disbelief. As I was about to leave the room, the second plane hit the other tower. I fell to my knees and prayed, knowing that this was a terror attack. I called Sandye. She was in the living room on the couch. A contractor was working on our back porch.

Sandye: "I can't believe it. I am watching it on TV now."

Kent: "I will call you later. Just pray."

I tried to call American Airlines for the meeting, but they were locked down. If I had left earlier, I would have been stuck there for a long time. The details were revealed and two of American Airlines' planes were lost with all those souls. I had to figure out how I was to get home, knowing the meeting was cancelled. Sandye called and told me to be very careful. The news said that the Sears Tower in Chicago was a target. Knowing that the planes would not fly for some time, I decided to keep my rental car and drive back to Atlanta. There was no other option and I figured that I could deal with the rental company later.

As I drove from one state to the next, I sensed an eerie quietness without planes in the air. A sonic boom scared me. I found out later that it was the president's plane returning to DC. I constantly talked to Sandye, who was in deep prayer through my entire trip. This was the one time in her life where she felt God's spirit so strongly that she spoke in tongues. She prayed for hours waiting for me. It was the longest eleven hours of my life waiting to get to Sandye and feel safe. Blinking signs in Atlanta were saying: "National Alert. All airports are closed." I have never seen the highways so empty during rush hour time. Upon arrival, I couldn't hug and kiss Sandye fast enough and tell her I loved her. God bless those families who lost loved ones. God was now entrenched in our lives.

Pastor Steve recommended that we start a home group and host a disciple class, designed to equip believers with the tools they need to lead others in their faith walk. Nine people came, four couples and the leader. We met every week for nine months and got to know each other very well. We always had food, studied together, and shared life's experiences. This was the first time I realized that people who attended church were not boring and were normal. Growing up, normal for me involved partying. The few times that I entered a church were not memorable.

About six months into the class, Sandye's father came down to visit. We talked about how Sandye stepped away from church and religion due to her father's sternness. Our class wanted to meet him.

Sandye: "Oh, I don't recommend we do that. He is very strong in his beliefs."

They remained adamant about meeting him. Then the time came and they were so happy to make the introduction. He stood five-foot-seven; a good-looking Italian man with a full head of grey hair that had slowly turned from black. He was not at all imposing. After sharing a meal, we stayed at the dining table and started the Bible study. We were discussing the meaning of a passage while several people were talking at the same time. Pete, sitting in the middle of the table, slammed his fist down on the table with a loud thud. The room deafened in shock.

Pete: "Now let me tell you what that means and you are all going to listen."

He proceeded to explain his opinion of the passage for fifteen minutes. No one said a word. Sandye sat in the corner shaking her head with a smile, knowing what was going to happen. Later, when we were alone with the class, one of the ladies who strongly wanted to meet Pete said:

Lady: "That man really scared me."

Sandye: "Welcome to my world. I told you. That is why we called our life, 'Living with the church of Pete.' We were expelled from many churches over the years."

Pete had very valid points, but his presentations were confrontational. In the same visit, he cornered me at the dinner table for about two hours discussing the Bible. When I finally got a reprieve, I asked Sandye, "Why didn't you jump in and help me?"

Sandye: "I wanted you to experience what my first eighteen

years were like. You only had two hours."

Although the experience seemed rough, we shared Godly stories later with joy. I realized that if I could share God's Word through love and example, then a lot more people would care to listen.

United Methodist churches regularly moved their pastors. I had no idea that Pastor Steve was about to be transferred to Augusta, Georgia. On his last day, the congregation was in tears saying their goodbyes. This man showed me God in a new and fresh light. Over the next month, we did not feel at home and started searching for a new church. We started attending Sugarloaf United Methodist Church in Duluth, Georgia. There we began attending a new small group headed by Leroy and Linda. They were a charismatic couple, infectiously positive to be around. Leroy was a renowned lawyer on a national stage.

We met together many times outside the church and they knew how to throw a great party. I was experiencing joy that I never thought possible within the bounds of a church. In that group, we met a man named, Wendall Tarkington. He visited us at our home and shared about playing Christian music twenty-four-seven in the house. He said that it would help during difficult days dealing with MS. We decided to try it, and it has had a positive impact ever since. There would be times when I would walk in the room frustrated and the song on the radio would change my world immediately. It blew my mind that contemporary Christian music could sound like the Rock and Roll music that I grew up to and at the same time give you a life long message. Our relationship with Wendall and his wife Peggy would continue for years to come.

I was travelling two to three weeks a month. During one trip to Mississippi, I called Sandye to see how she was doing.

Sandye: "You are not going to believe what happened last night. At three A.M. the house burglar alarm went off. It really scared me."

That surprised me, because Sandye never showed any fear.

Kent: "So, what did you do?"

Sandye: "I struggled to find my walker and get through the dark house. (not knowing if someone was in the house) As I was finding my way to the alarm pad, the phone started ringing. I must have taken too long to shut the alarm off. Then I took too long to get to the phone. A couple minutes later, the police arrived with the alarms blaring. We finally figured everything out but it set me back a bit."

Kent: "I'm so sorry, honey, that I was not there."

Sandye: "Me too." (trembling in her voice)

This made me think about what I should do next. I didn't want her to be in this position again, but I had no good answers. She moved on much better than me. I was starting to realize how vulnerable she was and that I could not always protect her.

Humor Break

In two-thousand-two, Sandye was transitioning from holding my hand and using a cane to relying on a walker. It was a frustrating time as she did not want to lose her independence. Struggling to walk was a battle for Sandye. I was usually working upstairs and the sound of a crash or some loud noise would send me reeling throughout the house looking for her. At times she would catch herself falling and try to brace herself on the walker without success. That was a time when she felt that her independence was fading. That thought was devastating. I would hear the sound of the walker slamming into the wall or something falling. Immediately, I would drop whatever I was doing to find her. On one occasion, I began to panic. I went from room to room shouting.

Kent: "Sandye! Sandye, where are you?"

Sandye: "Ugh! Gross, disgusting."

Kent: "Sandye, I'm coming."

Sandye: "Gross, Ugh."

Kent: "I hear you."

Sandye: "Yuck."

Following her voice and disgusted screams, I came upon her sitting in the dirty cat litter box.

Kent: (with a sense of relief) "Are you okay?"

Sandye: "It stinks."

Kent: "What happened?" (Sandye had a look of total disgust with fire in her eyes)

Sandye always had a keen sense of smell. The idea of sitting in a filthy litter box along with the stench destroyed her sensibilities. I will never forget that look of disgust and fire in her eyes and on her face. Although it may have only been a few minutes, to her it was an eternity.

Sandye: "Get me out of here. It stinks. Get me out of here. Take my clothes off and burn them."

Carefully, I stripped off her clothes and stuffed them into a large trash bag and threw them away. Later, as I told this story to many people, Sandye still has that same look of disgust and shear panic in her eyes when she relives that smell. Although, others would laugh with me hysterically, Sandye would relive the smelly experience all over again. I can still hear the "Ugh! Gross, disgusting" Thank God she has a good sense of humor.

***

It was now more difficult for Sandye to travel. With the large house, we invited the whole family for Thanksgiving dinner. There were twelve people. Sandye planned the whole dinner. I helped her cook it while my family partied. Our family usually never cooked. Our tradition was to travel and do an activity like skiing. Cooking was work and why would we choose to do that while on vacation. We asked my family to keep our tradition and stop what they were doing, write down five things they were thankful for. Usually, it was around noon. Every two hours we would have everyone share one item they were thankful for. One nephew, who was thirteen, to his mother's surprise, said that he was thankful for her. Aahs and Ooh erupted. On the comical side, his older brother was thankful for his TV. Sandye worked very hard to make the dinner special. She was finishing up with several items in the oven and excused herself.

> Sandye: "I'm going to change and freshen up for dinner. Keep an eye on the sweet potatoes. It's the last thing in the oven."

She grabbed her walker and slowly maneuvered to the bedroom to change. The five hours of work had taken its toll. My family talked at the same time without listening to each other including myself. We call it multi-tasking. We were all in the kitchen having a boisterous conversation while drinking beer.

> Kent's sister: "Is something burning?"

The sweet potatoes were black and smoking. Everyone thought it was funny, but my heart dropped. I knew I had to tell Sandye that I messed up. She looked so pretty and proud for all she had done that day. She shook her head in disbelief, knowing that her family treated holidays so different than mine. Her family's celebration involved cooking and helping each other. Most of the holiday was filled with joy in the kitchen while working together to create the perfect meal.

When we sat down to eat, Sandye smiled.

Kent: "Honey, are you going to eat anything?"

Sandye: "No, honey. Go ahead."

I knew that she was too tired to eat. Later in the bedroom, she asked me to get her a plate of whatever was left. Many of the items were gone and that weighed heavy on my heart. She was a great host and always ensured that her guests were cared for first.

Sandye's walking became harder. She held on to her walker with white knuckles. Many times, I would hear her stumble. As she would fall, she would slam the walker into the wall or TV. I held her up and ensured that she was ok.

Kent: "What are we going to do about this? How can I protect you?"

She had so much pride and did not want to be a liability for me.

Sandye: "Don't worry about it. I'll make do."

It was important that I kept my work separate from our personal life. She did not want to be a liability and did not want me to share her struggles with my work or family. As with many others with MS, she started to have internal stomach and bowel issues. Often, these would take hours to deal with. I learned patience in helping her through these times. Later, I learned that eighty percent of spouses are not able to handle these situations and leave the marriage. That frustrated me. I was determined to not be in that statistic. I couldn't believe that people would leave someone that they loved.

On another time away at work, Sandye had her own office in the front of the house. While sitting at her rolltop desk, she was doing her daily devotional. Her positive spirit drew her close to the Lord. She felt God's presence tell her to get up without using the walker and go to the kitchen for an apple. At this time there was no physical way possible that she could walk without the aid of a walker. She would fall immediately. Staying in the spirit, she pushed her way into a standing position. She kept praying and praising God, while starting to walk without the walker. She walked twenty feet into the kitchen without touching anything, praying the whole time. She took a cutting board out, cut up an apple, put it on a plate and then on a tray. She put both hands on the tray and walked back to her office praising God. Five feet from the desk she thought to herself, "Wow! I'm doing this." At that moment she collapsed to the floor. The tray flew in the air and the plate smashed. She started crying and felt like she dropped forty-thousand feet, landing in a gutter. She told me later that she pulled a Peter from the Bible. She had her eyes on the Lord like Peter walking on the water. When she looked away she began to fall, just as Peter sank in the water. Sandye yearned to get back with Jesus while she crawled over to her walker to pull herself up and sit down. It took her days to recover from that emotional experience.

Wendall was an elder at Sugarloaf UMC. He stated that Pastor Scott was very familiar with supernatural healing from his mission trips around the world. Wendall shared testimony about elders laying hands on the sick and performed healing ceremonies as stated in the Bible. He recommended that I talk to Pastor Scott. I made an appointment with him and shared Wendall's views. Sandye was open to any form of prayer for healing. Pastor Scott shared one event in Asia when he witnessed a powerful healing. He was willing to meet with us and members of our small group. We met after work and had a special prayer ceremony in the sanctuary. Following scripture, He anointed Sandye's head with oil. About twenty people prayed over Sandye for healing. I never felt anything like this but felt comfortable with the Holy Spirit in the room. Pastor Scott welcomed all prayers. Sandye did not show any signs of change at that moment. However, we left the church feeling a sense of love and comfort. We knew that God was in control. We had a feeling that Gods timing is not the same as ours.

I was traveling all over the country at this time calling on large accounts. On many trips I would get up ridiculously early to stay the previous night with Sandye. It would make the trip feel shorter for her. One morning I decided to get dressed in very low light in the bedroom as to not wake her. I hurried out to the airport and flew to Kansas City. I was meeting a large customer, known to be notorious for negotiating a tough deal. We were close to the end of the negotiating but she kept insisting our company give more and more money, if we wanted to keep the business. As in my tradition (even I would not know what I would do next) I responded.

> Kent: "You have taken the clothes off of my back, so you might as well have everything."

Leaning over, I took off my high-end black dress shoes and threw them on her desk.

> Kent: "We are all in on this deal! Now I have to go home with no shoes."

When I got dressed in the dark hours earlier, I had put on one black dress shoe with tassels and one without. We all looked a bit shocked.

Buyer: "Get those shoes off my desk. They don't even match."

Without a second thought, I grabbed the one shoe with tassels and ripped them off.

Kent: "Now they do. They're all yours!"

It got quiet in the office. There was an uncomfortable moment of silence. I was always taught that the next person that speaks loses in the final moments of a sale. So, I waited while my stomach was flipping over on the inside.

Buyer: "I have never seen anyone stand up to me like that. (she started to snicker) Take your shoes off my desk. We will accept the deal you offered. You sir have a lot of guts. I also see your passion and that you care."

Relieved that she didn't throw me out, we all started to laugh. The only one who was not laughing was my wife when I got home, because I had ruined my most expensive pair of shoes. But that event did not surprise her. I learned to incorporate my wild side with my professional side and people appreciated it. I later learned how to be more careful in taking calculated risks and that I needed to put emotions in check in a heated situation.

My good friend Ken Morris, a journeyman salesman in our industry, recommended me for a position with Foster Farms on the West Coast. I would still be covering the same area where I lived, but they were known for their great benefits, salaries and really talking care of their people. They were a family-owned organization. I flew to California and interviewed with seven people. They offered me the position. The day that I gave my two-week notice to leave the juice company, I was flying to DC. Ray, the CEO of the juice company, upon hearing that I gave my two weeks, met with his VP.

Ray: "Where is he? I want to go talk to him."

VP (BOB): "He's about ready to board a plane for DC."

When I got off the plane in Washington DC, Ray was waiting for me. He flew from Ohio and beat my plane there.

Ray: "You are not leaving my company. We have plans for you. Let's sit and talk."

We spent the rest of that day meeting, as my appointment was not until the next morning.

Ray: "I'm going to have Bob put together a package to keep you here with our company."

I was incredibly grateful and humbled by their actions. Bob took the next two weeks to convince me to stay. On my last scheduled day, I changed my mind and called Foster Farms with sorrow, due to my last-minute decision, that I would not take the position. I had to smooth it over with my friend Ken Morris, who had egg on his face with Foster Farms for recommending me. He was very nice about the whole situation. Bob and I became very close over the next year, and he followed through with the promise of a higher position with the company.

Sandye: "I am so proud that you have become the man that I prayed for."

I loved those words. My gambling habit nearly killed our relationship in the past. Now that part of my life is in the past. The one that I love sees me in a whole new light. What a blessing.

***

Chip, chip, chip. Spiritual growth removes more imperfections. Flexibility helps during difficult situations as well as humor. Impetuous behavior gets a lesson, but sincerity wins. Faith and trust begin to define me as God and Sandye have taught me.

Alaska Get Away

Trips were special to Sandye, but even more so when she could share them with other friends. When I started talking about an Alaskan cruise for my fortieth birthday, Sandye insisted that Brenda and Robert join us. Robert told me he could not afford it at the time. Keeping the promise that I made to Sandye in Paris to bring Brenda with us, I made the call and worked out all the details for that to happen. We made them an offer they could not refuse by using my airline points to pay for their flights. Robert wasn't thrilled about the idea of a cruise but decided to go anyway. Once again, I had extra points to upgrade the flights to first class. We were not in the air fifteen minutes when two juice drinks accidentally dumped in Sandye's lap. Despite her failing dexterity, she was not going to let that dampen the long trip ahead. We chose to laugh off those ridiculous situations and covered her pants with towels. Sandy had special long sleeve shirts designed for everyone to commemorate the trip. The shirts matched the original birthday shirts she got me for a birthday party twelve years prior. Her attention to detail blew my mind.

The first destination was Salt Lake City, Utah and then on to Anchorage. There, we would spend the night at a hotel and catch a shuttle bus early the next morning to Seward, where the cruise ship was docked. This was a long trip. When we arrived at the hotel, we saw great views in Anchorage and took beautiful pictures from the hotel bar. We were all tired when we arrived but Sandye's body was completely exhausted. It was all I could do to get her into the bed in the hotel room for the night in Anchorage. We we had to catch the shuttle at seven the next morning. At six-thirty I tried everything to wake her up.

> Kent: "Sandye, I need to help you put your clothes on. Brenda and Robert will be at the shuttle in twenty minutes. We cannot miss the trip to Seward where we will meet the cruise ship."

> Sandye: "Okay, lets get started."

Right in the middle of her sentence she would fall back into a deep sleep. This happened three times and I was at a loss. Even though her mind was working her body would shut down. Usually I would just let her sleep, but there was only one shuttle to Seward per day. If we missed it we might miss the cruise. I realized that in the future we needed to build in more time for every planned event for Sandye's body to catch up and alleviate our stress factors. I helped her get dressed while she was asleep and carried her onto the Shuttle. We drove for about an hour while she was sleeping comfortably on the shuttle bus. We passed a large lake with colorful planes with pontoons everywhere. It looked like a parking lot of cars waiting to take daily shoppers home to their Island. Alaska is drop dead beautiful every direction you look. The scenic view was spectacular as we travelled. Sandy was able to wake up in time to see some wildlife and glaciers.

We arrived in Seward and rented a house for the night, planning on catching the cruise ship the next day. We rented a car close to where the cruise ship was located. While in the Hertz rental car place, we looked out the window and saw the most gorgeous snow-peaked mountains in all four directions. There was a bald eagle perched on a post just outside. I spoke to an employee behind the desk.

Kent: "I cannot believe you have this view everyday at work."

Employee: "Why do you think I moved here, its like heaven and I do not want to wake up."

We all smiled knowing that we would never forget Seward, Alaska. We decided to drive in a national park, where you could walk up and get close to an actual glacier. While driving Sandye spotted something.

Sandye: "Hey that tourist place has huskie dogs. Let's pull over and check it out."

We were always up for an adventure. This place was called the Iditarod, where they trained the dogs to run in the famous Iditarod Dog Sled Race for hundreds of miles in the winter. When they train the dogs in the summer, they put wheels on the sleds to give the dogs a workout. To supplement their costs, they sold tickets to ride in the sled while the dogs were running. The huskies took off and the guide with the reins hollered signals. The dogs would run full speed around corners, over hills and down long paths. They were like a well oiled machine. I was holding Sandye tight so she wouldn't fall out. The girls screamed with joy as their hair blew in the cold crisp air. After the ride we were able to hold the puppies that were going to be superior athletic dogs one day. We were able to suggest names for the puppies. This was a moment in time that all four of us absolutely loved. It was a unique experience. We left and proceeded to the glacier, which was overwhelming once we got up close. We learned from a guide that the snow presses together so hard that it causes the color of the snow on the glacier to turn blue. We could see a climber way up this blue glacier. The guide said that it was dangerous and not recommended. We were looking at something you cannot really describe or appreciate unless you see it live. Thank you, Lord!

The next day Sandye was too tired to go hiking before we had to leave for the ship. Robert and Brenda went on a separate excursion. When they returned, they shared about their time.

Brenda: "We are so glad that you didn't come."

Kent: "Why?"

Brenda: "We went back to the same national park hiking trail towards the glacier. They closed the road the day before, due to a bear hunting a baby moose right by the tourists! The trail was opened back up for us, but we encountered a bear anyway. We took a video of the bear coming out on the trail following right behind us. It scared us to death."

Kent: "Sandye may have been dead meat in her wheelchair."

Brenda: "You got it."

We counted our blessings and headed for the cruise ship. Seward is a small town by a small lake called Resurrection Bay. This bay is attached to the inside passage river that goes all the way down to Vancouver. When looking at the size of the bay before the ship arrived you could not believe that a 2000-person ship would fit in that small water space. The depth of the water was actually 972 feet, which was unbelievable. We had not boarded the ship yet and already we had a trip of a lifetime.

Celebrity Cruise Lines are known for their exceptional food and the first night on board was a formal dinner. We started to get ready an extra hour and a half early, so that I could help Sandye get ready and then myself. The four of us were seated with six other people that were from around the country. Our group included an older couple who had been on many cruises, a younger couple who were world travelers and two sisters from New Jersey. They soon realized that we were wound up for our trip and that they were going to have fun. We ordered steak, lobster and Baked Alaska. The dinner was amazing.

Robert: "We have to break this table in right."

He brought out a plastic bag and dumped packages containing individual big plastic red clown lips. When you would wear them, it looked like you had a funny smile on your face. Everyone joined in and took a picture with their lips on, along with the dining staff. They all knew we were in for a festive week.

The cruise boats in Alaska travel on the inside passage. This allows you to see humongous snowcapped glaciers right in front of you, one after another. We did not have to do anything as the ship guided its way past one postcard majestic scene after another. Words cannot express the beauty. We viewed for hours.

Brenda: "We need to go to sleep, it's getting late."

Sandye: "It can't be. It's light outside."

Kent: "I cannot believe it is 2:30 in the morning and it looks like 3 in the afternoon. We better go to bed or we'll never get up to see Skagway."

Parts of Alaska get nineteen hours of sunlight a day in the Summer, Wow!

Due to the drastic temperature changes during the summer months, we had to dress in many layers. We were able to take a gorgeous train ride in Skagway and went to the local hangouts in Juneau. Everything was so different from our past and felt like we were in a whole different country. When we got to Sitka, it was my actual fortieth birthday. Sandye gave us the t-shirts that she copied from my 28th birthday.

Sandye: "I only made four shirts this time but they had to be long sleeved."

All four of us promptly put on our shirts pictured with an Alaskan party fish. We were going out on a boat to see if we could spot whales. As we floated along on a small boat, out of the water came the monstrous elegant beast.

Sandye: "Look Kent, there is your birthday fish!"

I was moved beyond comprehension. We returned to the ship and went to dinner on a high that would last for days.

Elder Gentleman at our table: "Happy Birthday Kent. Where did your excursion go today?"

Kent: "Thank you. It was the best day ever. We saw eleven whales at a very close distance. What did you all do?"

"Oohs and Ahhhs" came from the table audience.

Elder Gentleman: "It was great. We took a helicopter ride to the top of a glacier and then rode a dog sled back to the bottom of the mountain."

"WOW!" Everyone was enchanted.

Sisters from NJ: "Our tour was on a river boat and we saw hundreds of Bald Eagles everywhere."

Young couple: "We went fishing and caught a huge three-foot Salmon. As we were reeling it in, a bear stole it off our line, which we were glad to relinquish."

Our six tablemates now shared special over the top experiences, building new long-term friendships. We were all blown away at the grandeur of Alaska and that we were just small participants in nature's domain. God's majesty was everywhere. The color was magical.

The next day our ship pulled up to a glacier where icebergs were floating everywhere. Some ice was breaking off the glacier which they called "calving." It was something that I had never seen before and probably wouldn't get the chance again. In Ketchikan, we saw carved totem poles everywhere.

We left Vancouver, which has one of the largest, gorgeous city parks on its island. You could look back across the water and see the spectacular view of the Vancouver skyline. Then we drove a rental car back to Seattle where we would fly back home. At the border, I realized that I had misplaced my passport.

Robert: "We are going to have to leave you in Canada Kent."

They were snickering behind my back while I worried. In 2002 it was not as much of a big deal and they let me into the United States without a problem. I found the passport in a pocket in my suitcase ten years later. We went up to the top of the Space Needle in Seattle and once again wanted to freeze every moment in our memory as we scanned the city.

Robert changed his tune about the experience of the cruise. He talked about the food, the beer, but mostly the whole majestic experience. It was the best thing he had ever done. If you ever had a doubt about a cruise or Alaska, just take a chance, and let God surprise you. Sharing those times of joy with close friends was very special to Sandye. She would rather watch them experience life events for themselves, than to try communicating her experiences. To her, words were not adequate to express moments of great joy.

***

Chip, chip, chip. The sculptor appeared to laugh when some of the chips fell. Sharing special moments and humor with friends does amazing things for the soul. Understanding that God cares about every aspect of our lives, adds to my faith and trust in Him.

Texas Giving

Bob, the VP of the Juice company, came to me nine months later.

Bob: "Kent, if I leave this company. Would you ever want to work with me again?"

Kent: "If you went to a dog food company, I would follow you."

Bob snickered, but he knew that I was faithful to people. He left the company three months later and joined a new organization. Legally was not allowed to pursue me. Later, I called the new company, which sold jalapeno peppers out of New Mexico, to see if they had any open positions. They said it was great timing. They needed someone to head their food service division. Sandye believed in me and my decisions.

Bob left the juice company six months earlier. I reached out to him, knowing that he might have plans for me. I went to Deming, New Mexico, (near El Paso, Texas) to interview and had a rude awakening. It was a very different culture. it was just a few miles from the Mexican border. I wanted to work for Bob, so I took the position. I headed the food service division with two people reporting to me. I covered the whole country calling on large customers. I was now a big fish in a small pond. A new CEO from

Del Monte named, Norm, came to the company. I hit it off with him, but he was very volatile. He drank a lot, and you did not want to get on his bad side the next day after he partied. Four letter words were flying everywhere. After a year working with the CEO, I was offered a VP position and a move to Dallas. This was the dream title that I always thought I wanted, and Sandye was always open for change.

The company moved us from Georgia to Texas. It was a hard pill to swallow for Russ and Leslie. We had eight years of holiday traditions and now that would end. On our trip to the airport, we had two cats. One was named, Cleo, which Brenda purchased as a kitten for Sandye, the other was named Sydney. The cats kept leaving the containers that we kept them in while driving down to the airport. We rushed to the pet supply store enroute to the airport and bought a better cage. Going through security was like a travelling road show. Sandye had her wheelchair, walker and someone assisting her. I had the cat carrier and luggage. The TSA employee told me to remove the cats and hand carry them through the detector. I looked at him like he was crazy.

Kent: "Are you sure you want me to do that? What if they get loose and run all over?"

TSA: "Those are the rules, sir. You must comply."

Hoping the cats would not scratch, I firmly grabbed them behind their necks. With a cat in each hand, I walked through security. Another TSA employee unexpectedly turned and saw two cats. He freaked out. It was hilarious. Sandye was getting patted down at the same time. We learned that travelling was going to be a whole new story. When we got to the plane, all the passengers were on board. There were special chairs for wheelchair people to move down the aisle. Sandye was hitting people due to the tight space (usually we would board before everybody else, but this time we were running behind). She was able to slide into her seat, while I had to find a place for the cats. Originally, I planned to put the cats under the seat, but the new cage was too large. I felt like everyone on the plane was waiting for me to get seated and were staring, I found an open luggage overhead compartment. Just as I went to put the cats in, a flight attendant tapped me on the shoulder.

> Attendant: (Squealy voice) "You can't put those cats in the overhead. What are you doing?"

I felt like I had just been caught by the Vice Principal of my school.

> Kent: "They won't fit under the seat. Where do you want me to put them?"

Some people laughed. Others were angry. At this point I was sweating and didn't care if the cats made it on the plane.

> Attendant: "Let's go up to the pilot and figure it out."

We ended up placing the cats in the luggage compartment under the plane. Thank God, when we arrived in Texas, they were ok, but a little beat up. Sandye would have never forgiven me if those cats were not ok.

This trip was a huge lesson for future trips. No matter what, give yourself hours of extra time and plan for things to happen that might cause delay. It pays to be early and lowers the stress dramatically. Also plan on things to not go as planned.

I was moved to Texas as a vice-president in sales. I hit the ground running selling Jalapeno peppers. This was the first time that I worked from an office. This was a big change for Sandye as well, but she was up for it. I drove forty-five minutes to work. My office was nice with a window view. I was concerned about feeling like a caged lion. From the time that I left the elevator, I would stop at everyone's office enroute. Each day that would take forty-five minutes. I wasn't used to being in a solitary spot. This gave me a great chance to draw near to the senior VP and CEO.

Humor Break

This was the first time that I ever worked in an office away from home. Sandye was determined to lead a normal life while I was gone during the day. She helped with the construction of a pool in the back yard and resumed weekly physical therapy. She routinely woke up early to see me off to work. On this particular day I came back from work after nine hours and entered the front door. I looked to the right in her office. There she was on the floor sitting Indian style looking at a stack of papers. There were small stacks of papers all over the room on the floor. It looked like her office had moved to the ground. The phone, paper clips, scissors, drink, and food were in their place on the carpet. Her rocker was pushed off to the side. At first, I was very alarmed. Something didn't feel right, but it was well organized.

Kent: "Sandye, what's going on?"

Sandye; "I wasn't strong enough to push myself off the floor and onto the walker. I had a lot of things to do today. So, I did them." (said, matter-of-factly)

Kent: "How long have you been on the floor?" (knowing that
it had to have been several hours)

Sandye: "Oh. A little while."

Kent: "Why didn't you call me?"

Sandye: "We all have a job to do. It was no big deal."

I shook my head, chuckled, and helped her get off the floor. I thought,
"How could this lady, who struggled so hard, shrug off such difficult
situations so easily? I couldn't help but think how much I loved her for
trying so hard and never complaining. Acting as it never happened, she
moved on to the next topic.

***

Sandye: "It's time that I got into that jacuzzi by the pool."

It took a couple of years to build the inground pool and jacuzzi with a
fountain in the middle. Sandye put her swimsuit on, which was a monu-
mental task. She maneuvered her way onto the back porch, moving slowly.
I moved in front of her to assist. I started backing up. We got to the jacuzzi.
I pushed the walker away and supported her with my arms. As I backed up,
we walked in step. I was moving backwards while she was going towards

me. She had not been in the water for two years and couldn't wait to get in. As we entered the Jacuzzi, there was a built-in cement seat. I was planning to step onto the seat and have her follow. As I stepped back, I stepped too far. I fell straight back. The fountain in the middle was a small plastic tube shooting water straight up. My backside snapped the tube in half. As I was falling, Sandye was holding both of my arms. She started to fall as well. It was almost like she was doing a full face-first dive into nothing but cement.

The fear raged through my body, knowing that she had to have cracked her head open. As I came up out of the water, I flailed my arms in an attempt to reach her. After locating her body, I pulled her up as quick as possible. I was expecting to see blood everywhere and had horrible thoughts. As her face came out of the water, in complete shock, I thought she was badly injured. Miraculously, she was not harmed.

Kent: "Are you hurt?"

Sandye: (looking really upset) "You got my hair wet."

My heart leaped out of my chest because I knew that you could dive into that pool a hundred times and be hurt ninety-nine of them.

Sandye: "Get me out of this water. I'm cold."

It took a while to get her back into the house and comfortable. That was the only time she had any experience with the pool while we lived there. The pool was originally built for her. It did provide a nice profit on the house when we sold it. Pools are great therapy for people with disabilities but it was too hard for Sandye to participate. So we moved on.

We got settled in a suburb of Dallas and knew that we needed to locate a church. A new United Methodist church was starting in a middle school. The pastor was very nice and he also led the worship. The congregation was small. We were one of the first members in the first ninety-days of its existence. They were trying to plant it and make it grow. It was exciting to be part of a new church. We became friends with many of the members and became part of their local projects.

At one meeting, a local gentleman in the horse industry, spoke about his project that involved retired racehorses. His group provided equine therapy for autistic people. This usually cost a hundred-fifty dollars per hour, but it was his mission to provide over two-hundred fifty lessons each week for free. His name is Charles Fletcher. Seeing Sandye and her disability, he thought it could help her as well. Riding a horse could help improve her abdominal muscle strength. Sandye visited the horse farm with me and another lady from church. She was able to climb aboard Holly, a beautiful white horse, from a special platform made for her. There were no saddles. Sandye's body felt the horse. They walked for about a half hour. Afterwards, you could see that it helped her. One instructor told her that some autistic people spoke their first words while riding these horses. When Sandye was finished, I could tell that her body was worn out. As we lifted her off the platform, from the short, stocky horse, she spoke with a very straight face meaning every word.

Sandye: "That's the biggest thing that I have had between my legs in a long time."

The lady from the church was howling in laughter.

The school, where the church service was held, offered a convenience for Sandye. It was extremely accessible. Her wheelchair could easily take her to the front where she could pull herself up and stand with the congregation. Being part of a new church was a rewarding experience.

In keeping our holiday traditions, we found a local church that was serving Thanksgiving meals for the homeless. They also had set up delivery meals for poor communities. One day before the event, we were driving past a trailer park when Sandye yelled.

Sandye: "Wait. Turn around, go back, and turn in there."

As we pulled into the park, we were on an uneven dirt road with large potholes. These trailers were run down and rickety.

Sandye: "I can't believe my eyes. People actually live in these homes and it's only a half-block from a subdivision with five-hundred-thousand-dollar houses. We cannot be blind to this need."

The road caused me to be concerned for our car and our safety.

Sandye: "We need to find out how many meals that these homes need."

We went door to door, asking people if they would like meals and took a count. One double-wide trailer had eleven people living inside. Our count was over fifty meals. When Thanksgiving arrived, Sandye was serving cranberry sauce. I was next to her serving rolls. It was very busy. Sandye was falling behind because her hands were not working properly. I tried to help her by serving cranberry sauce.

Sandye: "Hey! Mind your own. I'm cranberry and your roll."

I found my place. We took the meals out to the park. I carried the meals into one home where a little boy, wearing only his underwear, was covered in dirt. The lady told me to put the meals on the counter. There was no room with all the clutter. When I got back to the car while Sandye was waiting, I was choked up.

Kent: "How do these kids ever have a chance in life."

Sandye: "That is why someone has to help them and that is us."

The next summer, Sandye wanted to get electric fans for all of those trailers. She negotiated with different companies. A manager at Sears worked out a deal with her and she bought thirty fans. It was a hundred degrees for ninety straight days. Sandye was going to help them one way or another. That was another lifechanging experience for me in learning how to give.

Dr. Stuart in Atlanta recommended a neurologist, Dr. Frohman, who worked at the university's teaching hospital in Dallas. He was MS certified. The first time we met, Sandye connected well. There was no topic that we could not discuss. At times Dr. Frohman would bring in five doctor trainees and ask very tough questions. No question was off limits. During that time, I was extremely quiet. Sandye would fire back with witty responses and everyone laughed. During this time, Sandye's symptoms were causing her feet and hands to be very numb. An average person would feel like they were asleep. Dr. Frohman was willing to try any new medication, even though there was nothing available to stop the MS progression. He asked Sandye if she was willing to try a drug called, cytoxin, a chemotherapy drug which was normally used for cancer. She tried it for nine months. The side effects were horrible, causing her to be sick for long periods of time.

A new drug for MS called, tysabre, came out. The main affect was that it halted the formation of lesions, causing her to feel better. She was on this drug for six months and it seemed to have dramatic results. Then a few patients across the country, who were taking it, were diagnosed with PML, a bad brain disease. The FDA pulled it off the market and it was no longer available. We were back to square one. Without any solution available we felt disheartened. We decided to make every vacation trip we took be the absolute best and the next trip of a lifetime knowing that tomorrow is not promised.

Border Foods primarily sold jalapeno and chili peppers. Chili peppers are a huge business in New Mexico and Texas. The largest customer was based in Albuquerque, New Mexico. His name was Larry. He owned his own distribution center and thirteen Mexican restaurants. Up until now, Larry did not do business with us and our CEO, Norm, really wanted that business. I challenged Norm and said that if I could land two-million dollars' worth of business, would he agree to send Larry, his partner and me to an all-expense paid trip to Pebble Beach to play golf. Pebble Beach and Augusta are a golfer's dream destinations.

Norm: "I'll take that challenge. You go get the business and don't fail."

After six months of negotiations with Larry, we sat at his desk in an old paneled office. Larry pulled a bottle of Tequila.

Larry: "I always settle a deal with a drink."

I thought, when in Rome, I need to do this thing. We had the drink, shook hands, and enjoyed an unbelievable trip to play Pebble Beach. Norm was elated. I was in hog heaven.

From the lessons learned from playing Christian music twenty-four seven, we picked up a local Dallas station. They partnered with Chick Fil-A during the holidays. For the month of December, the station broadcasted from a different franchise. They asked people to complete a survey for things that they needed and asked listeners to come to the live broadcast or examine the needs online. We thought this was a great idea and went down to the station. We began looking through many notebooks of needs listeners had sent in from around the city and selected three different wishes to grant. The first one was a lady named Virginia. She was in a wheelchair and lost one of her legs. Her niece wrote in and said that she really loved her aunt. She hoped that her aunt could get a microwave. We couldn't believe that she only wanted a microwave, so we chose her. After talking to some people at our church, one lady offered a handmade quilt. We decided to purchase holiday dinner items, got a gift card, and the microwave. We called the niece and planned to meet them both at Virginia's home. She lived in a small two room house. Virginia opened the door. Her niece was with her mother behind Virginia. She was a little elderly lady who pushed herself with one leg in a wheelchair, and a big smile came to her face.

Virginia: 'Did I win? Did I win?"

Kent: "Yes, you won. Thanks be to God."

We placed the quilt on her lap, the groceries on the table, and set up her microwave. We shared how much her niece must have loved her to write in to the station with that wish. Her niece, who was about thirteen, threw her arms around Virginia telling how much she loved her. As we drove away we said, "Look what God just did, this is great fun and could get addictive!"

The second lady was in a mall parking lot. She wrote in for coats for her children. Not knowing the preferences and sizes, we bought gift cards. We met her at her car. Three small children were in the back seat. She was timid and got out of the car. We introduced ourselves and gave her two gift cards plus a lot of groceries. It was quick. We got back in the car and glanced over. The lady was in tears. She had her hands in the air praying to God. It filled our hearts.

The last recipient was about two and a half hours away. A lady wrote in for her nephew who had cancer. Usually, we wouldn't drive that far, but her letter touched us deeply. The boy was still sick after months of chemo. The writer asked for him to have a good Christmas and the parents had very little. As we entered the house, many family members came over to greet us, acting like it was a great surprise. The boy did not know we were coming. A smile came to his tired face. The treatments had taken all his hair and strength. A child's joy beamed in his face when he saw a specific toy. For that moment he was cancer free. We added more wrapped presents as well as groceries. The boy's mother and aunt broke down in tears as we left. The joy God can bring through caring hearts is enormous. The radio station made this a huge event for the city of Dallas. Corporate sponsors provided jobs, vehicles, and much more. Even the disc jockeys cried.

***

Chip, chip, chip. Opening the heart towards the needs of others is a tremendous character builder. God even cares for pet cats. Often God leads us to new places to face needs, touch hearts, and share those experiences later. Good things happen when God leads. The artist spends a lot of time working on the heart, including mine as I vowed to keep my commitment to support and never leave her.

Back to Georgia

After two years in Dallas, we realized that the heat was too much for Sandye. Four straight months of a hundred degrees meant Sandye had to stay inside. I requested to work from home twice a week to make it easier on her. This put a stress in my relationship with my CEO, Norm. He was now an alcoholic and was not happy with the situation. I realized that it was more important to find the right people to work for than a big title position, or more money. My perspective was changing about what was truly important. The owners of the company fired Norm shortly thereafter. Even though the work conditions improved, Sandye's condition was getting much more difficult. We knew that we had to move back to Atlanta and surround ourselves with a good support system both at home and at work. I called my old boss from Minute Maid, Pam, who was now working for Schwans. On that day she was about to make an offer to another candidate after two months of negotiations.

Pam: "Are you serious? If I pull the plug on an offer at the last second, you better be ready to come back."

I started to realize that something far greater than me was in charge of our destiny and timing.

I was ready to take a reduction in pay and position to get what was best for Sandye. Working for Pam offered a comfort zone, knowing what was best for Sandye. Plus, I felt very comfortable with her boss Jim Swystell, our Vice President with Schwans. What a change from my previous addictive compulsive President to a man that was stable! Jim did not ever say anything bad about people. He was positive and stable. This was someone I wanted to follow. Soon after, we had a large meeting at Schwans where two large divisions merged together, and Jim was put in charge over both. This was the first meeting where most of the people would meet Jim. At the meeting Jim introduced himself.

> Jim: "Hello, my name is Jim Swystell, I try to keep my life in a priority. God first, family second, and work third. Sometimes I get it out of order but that is my goal."

I found this speech a risky approach for meeting a whole new management team. He did not compromise his morals and values based upon what other people would think. I would never forget this stand he made and hope to be like him.

The actual move from Texas to Atlanta was almost impossible for Sandye to handle physically and mentally. Someone with a nerve disease cannot handle pressure well. In Sandye's case her body tends to collapse. I did my best to keep her calm and isolate her while the move was taking place, I knew that this move was incredibly hard on Sandye. It would be next to impossible to ask her body to do this again. A interior designer friend of hers in Atlanta, named Sheila, helped us find a home near where we used to live. We needed a finished basement for caregiving. The basement was unfinished, but we had a plan in mind to complete the work. After seeing Sandye's condition, Sheila couldn't handle the progression of MS. We lost her and others as friends due to their responses to Sandye's condition and we hated it. New friends needed to be very flexible. I just did not realize that so many people could not or would not help when we needed it. They were just not equipped to handle the progressive disease changes. They wanted to help but most of them backed away. We looked forward and tried not to judge anyone.

After we got settled, Sandye needed time to recoup. This was much harder on her than ever before. We were excited to rejoin our small group at the Sugarloaf UMC, led by Leroy and Linda. The group knew we were coming but did not know when we would show up. They had not seen us in a month or more. The group met before the church service. When we arrived, the church had undergone remodeling. The meeting room was in a new building, and we were unaware of where to go. To get Sandye out of the car to the wheelchair, I needed to lift her, pivot and set her back down. This took a while to master. I pushed her down the new building's hallway, not knowing where to stop. We could hear a group at the end of the hall. Nearing the door, I could hear Leroy's boisterous jovial voice and knew that we were where we should be. The door was open and we rolled in hollering.

Kent: "HONEY! HONEY! We're home."

Twenty people roared, cheering to the extent that it was almost embarrassing. It was one of the best feelings ever. It was finally good to be where people made us feel like we were home.

After the holidays, Sandye was having major internal problems. I would try to help her for six hours to go to the bathroom. This was a major test for both of us. We went to a surgeon, who recommended a major surgery on both her bladder and bowels. This would mean that she would have tubes and a bag leaving her body constantly, but it would relieve the problems of the past years. It weighed heavily on her heart to make these physical changes and her thoughts of being feminine. We needed to do this for a more functional life. The surgery went well, but she had to stay at Piedmont hospital for eight days. I put a mattress on the floor next to her bed. The hospital had high quality service. The staff even wore tuxedoes. One night, a nurse could not wake Sandye up. She was shaking her, calling out her name, and ready to hit the emergency button for additional help. I knew that from past experiences, Sandye was in a deep sleep and needed it. The fatigue with MS required much more sleep. I stepped in front of the nurse and told her that it would be okay. Knowing she could lose her job, she responded.

Nurse: (looking in my eyes) "Are you sure?"

Kent: "Absolutely. If you wake her now. You will hurt her more than help her."

The nurse thought about it for a second and then backed off. Sandye slept another ten hours. She was okay. I learned that I needed to always be her advocate, and in many situations. I knew what was best for her due to past experiences. It was my job to guide the health professionals.

After a few weeks at home, our church had many people delivering food. Sandye did not feel like eating, but I put on some pounds. One time, two ladies from our group came with food. We knew Sally but we did not know the other lady named Margie. The four of us were talking in the living room.

Margie: "You have a beautiful place here on the golf course.

At home we call it the golf ball field (snickering), It looks like we could have a lot of fun if I came to visit again."

Kent: "You are not allowed to visit unless we have a really good time."

Margie: "I can have fun. I will dance and you need a lot of dollar bills to put in my skirt."

Sandye loved her response. Margie treated her like a normal person and she was joyfully youthful. They hit it off very quickly. She would routinely come over during Sandye's recuperation. One time, I was looking around the house for them. They were not in their usual hangout. I heard voices coming from the bathroom. I opened the huge walk-in closet doors. Sandye was sitting in her wheelchair with Margie sitting on a chest.

Margie: "This is our office. You need an appointment to come in. Get out and leave us alone. (both girls were smirking) Close the door when you leave."

I retreated, knowing that they were truly enjoying each other's company. I think they stayed another three hours and many more office hours later. They became very close friends. Margie helped us both have joy through the journey. She is an old soul with a youthful spirit.

On another occasion, Sandye was going through extensive work with a physical therapist who came to our home. Many friends and acquaintances knew that she was trying to recover strength through exercising. Because she wasn't improving, many also thought that she was not trying hard enough. That was not the case; her legs would not respond because of her progressive MS disease. This specific therapist was new and only knew what her medical textbooks told her, which said she would not be able to walk.

Therapist: "What are your personal goals, Sandye?'

Sandye: "I'm going to walk."

Therapist: (astounded) "Sandye, that's not a realistic goal. You will never walk."

That was the end of the conversation that week. It was time for the therapist to leave. You can't tell Sandye that you can't do something, and the word "never" is not in her vocabulary. This fueled her defying spirit. She was driven to prove this therapist wrong. On the morning when the therapist was scheduled to arrive, Sandye sat down in her walker and had me push her around the corner from the front door. Then she asked me to go upstairs to work. I had not seen her have strength to stand up or walk in months. The therapist rang the doorbell.

Sandye: "Come in."

As the therapist walked down the hallway towards Sandye, with every fiber and strength of her body, she fought and pushed herself into a standing position. She gripped the walker until her knuckles turned white, defying all logic to stand up. With all her might she fought to walk small steps around the corner. Seeing this, the therapist, stopped in her tracks, and was astounded and appeared to turn white. She thought she was looking at a ghost. Sandye did that just to prove a point. Later she shared the moment with me.

Kent: (laughing) "I would have liked to have seen her face."

Sandye: "You would have lost it, honey. It was great."

Often, when things seemed to get more difficult, humorous moments helped us laugh during the struggles. This was also an example of Sandye's will and that you could never tell her that she couldn't do something. Never underestimate the human will. Soon after, she stood up with the walker in front of Margie one last time. We would need an electric wheelchair for her to maneuver around in the future.

The insurance covered the cost of the electric chair. Sandye fought hard to not be in a wheelchair but realized the newfound independence that it now gave her. A friend built a ramp from the garage into the house. While practicing with the heavier wheelchair, I heard a loud banging sound. Before I could yell down to see if she was ok, I heard Sandye laughing.

Sandye: "Whoops. Wow! This is fun."

I hurried downstairs to see about the commotion. The powerful 415 lb wheelchair had ripped a kitchen cabinet door off, and it was on the floor.

Sandye: "Look at what this smooth machine did." (still laughing)

We knew we had to be very careful with the new chair. Sandye had backed into the jacuzzi so many times, that she created a large hole in the tile. She joked about trying to dig a hole to China. Around the house were many dents about waist high caused from the wheelchair. This chair could easily break your toes if it ran over them. I cried one time when it ran over my toes and was determined to not let that happen again.

***

Chip, chip, chip. Sandye's trials continue to build my patience. The move back to Georgia was part of God's plan. Times of joy restore my confidence in a loving God and have blessed my heart. The artist knew that the work would take a long time. Once again, humor was used to help make the journey more enjoyable.

Scary Moments

While in Tennessee working for Schwans, Margie was planning on stopping by to see Sandye around five o'clock after completing her business. She was on her way to Athens, Georgia. About twenty minutes past our home something told her to call Sandye. It was about 1:00 PM. She called twice with no answer. She told her husband to turn around and proceed to our house.

Husband: "Are you sure as it will delay us at least an hour?"

Margie: "I am deeply troubled by this feeling. Take me back right now."

Margie had the garage door keypad code, so she used it to enter the house. She opened the kitchen door and hollered Sandye's name. There was no response. She hurried across the house to the bedroom. She opened the door but Sandye was not there and not answering. This alarmed Margie because she knew that Sandye was supposed to be there. Margie started to search the main floor where Sandye could maneuver her wheelchair. She saw the electric wheelchair in the master bathroom near a sink. Sandye was upside down held by her seatbelt.

Margie: "SANDYE!" (screaming)

Sandye was unconscious. Margie had no idea if she was alive or not. She ran to the car and screamed for her husband to help her. They were able to undo her seatbelt and get her back in the chair, though she had passed out. They put cold water and ice on her and she woke up. They moved her onto the bed. After an hour or two, Margie called me.

Margie: "Sandye's OK. Now let me tell you what happened. Sandye told me that she was leaning over to get something from under the sink and fell forward. The seatbelt caught her but she was hung up. While hanging upside down, she couldn't breathe very well. The seatbelt pushed against her stomach. She couldn't reach anything under the sink. She prayed, 'Lord, I guess this is it'."

If Margie had not turned around and come to the house three hours later, liked originally planned, Sandye would not be with us today. Now, I was dealing with a new reality involving an electric wheelchair. It weighs four-hundred pounds and can be dangerous. Sandye was fearless with the new wheelchair. It gave her a sense of power and speed. She would take off in Costco and I had to run to catch up.

One time we went to a Joyce Meyers conference in the area. Afterwards, we were waiting in the parking garage for all the traffic to move. It was backed up into the garage. Sandye looked up and saw a long ramp where all the cars had left the area. To her this was a great opportunity to have some fun. She zoomed up the ramp, while I screamed.

Kent: "Where are you going?"

Sandye: "Don't worry about me."

I could barely see her in the distance. As she came into view, I could now see her clearly. About half the distance, I could see her moving at a rapid rate bouncing joyously. That really worried me, because she didn't have a seatbelt on, knowing that one wrong move could cause trouble. She flew by me, and I gasped.

Kent: "I'm glad you got that out of your system. You freaked me out."

Sandye: "That was so much fun. I'm going to do it again."

Off she went back up the ramp. I just had to hold my breath and let her be herself. On the second return down the ramp, I stopped her.

Kent: "The traffic is gone. It's time to leave."

On another occasion at the nail salon, I went to get the van. It had started to rain. She was about seventy-five feet away under a covered sidewalk. I lowered the ramp and waited inside for her to reach the van. She was cruising side to side until the ramp was down, like she was having fun and playing some type of game with the wheelchair. Then she straightened out and headed directly at me. Her head was down with a competitive look on her face heading straight for the ramp. When I realized that she wasn't slowing down, I screamed.

Kent: "Hey! What are you doing?"

She was barreling towards the van at the top speed, thinking that she could fly straight onto the ramp and stop on a dime to surprise me. The wheelchair wrenched to the side and launched Sandye onto the pavement into a pool of water. I jumped out and thought she was severely hurt but she was ok; just a bit dazed. I was able to get the wheelchair freed up. I loaded her and the chair into the van. Her hair was wet and her freshly trimmed nails needed repair. She had a disgusted look on her face. It was probably one of the maddest moments that I ever felt towards her.

Kent: "Don't ever do that again. What were you thinking?"

There was an eerie silence in the van the rest of the trip home. She looked like a wet puppy, with her lower lip out. What was supposed to be fun luckily did not turn tragic. This was another one of those amazing times when she didn't get hurt. I know that she was just having fun, but she was learning her limitations and the pressures of what she could handle. I have heard about guardian angels and, perhaps, she had one close by continually.

Margie decided to move to Florida to be near her grown children. She came by to offer comfort to Sandye. She shared that she would always be there for her. I made a deal with Margie that if she wanted to visit, I would pay for her ticket. Over the years, Margie took me up on my offer about two times per year. Every time she came back it was like she never left. They have so much fun together. We were now surrounding ourselves with people who could handle our situation in a positive uplifting environment.

Since we returned to Atlanta, we wanted to keep ties with the Dallas specialist, Dr. Frohman, who was willing to try new experimental drugs. We flew back and forth to Dallas once a year. Sandye tried different drugs that were very helpful for many MS patients, but some had dangerous side effects. This resulted in Sandye's body going through a lot of volatility. We flew back to see the Dr. Frohman in Dallas where Sandye exploded about the side effects. Her emotional outbursts were out of character and caused severed relationships with close friends. Losing her ability to walk played a major part in her emotional turmoil along with the pain and headaches due to the side affects of MS.

That resulted in a referral back to Dr. Stuart in Atlanta. We felt like Dr. Frohman would be with Sandye's journey throughout, but God had a better plan. The MS clinic headed by Dr. Stuart was recognized as the largest in the country and one of the best clinics in the world. We started working with various specialists at the clinic. One recommendation came from a family counselor whom we met in 1995 and was still working with Dr. Stuart. He told us to change our shower to a roll-in accessible one. Up to this point, I needed to lift Sandye out of her seat and over a threshold onto a chair in the shower. The MS organization helped fund the construction that made our lives better and easier to take a shower.

***

Chip, chip, chip. Perceived scary moments that end without harm further taught me that God is in control. The words, "Let go. Let God," remind me constantly of that fact when I start to fear. I can almost hear Him laughing with each incident as if to say, "Gotcha." Organizations are available to help if we look for them. The artist smiles.

Italy Trip of a Lifetime

As I looked down at my beautiful bride in the hospital room, there was an overwhelming peace over her body. It was just me and her yet it seemed like time was standing still. She had now been incoherent for one hour and fifteen minutes. In somewhat of a desperate plea, I told Sandye.

Kent: "We have so many things to see and do yet."

I smiled as I thought back to the trip we had taken to Italy. What an amazing trip of a lifetime!

Kent: "Do you remember Sandye? I remember every moment."

My mind went back about ten years to 2007.

Two years after we returned from Texas to Atlanta, we decided to celebrate Sandye's fiftieth birthday in a special way. I had built up enough travel points to update four flights to Europe. Our dear friends, Brenda and Robert, were not able to afford it, but Sandye insisted that they share the excitement. The plan was for Sandye and me to fly to Milan, Italy, for the first week; then travel to meet Brenda and Robert in Venice for a cruise. We left a week early, but before leaving, Margie flew up to help Sandye pack with a host of medical items and necessary clothing. She rolled up clothes into small balls and packed four large suitcases, along with, two travel bags, a walker and a wheelchair. We had not figured out how to manage all those items travelling across Europe. We constructed a system to maneuver our luggage and handicapped equipment through the airport. I am sure that we caused eyes to turn from our makeshift contraptions. My left hand was pushing Sandye in the wheelchair while she was guiding the walker in front of her. At the same time I was dragging our smaller carry on luggage with my right hand. It looked odd but we made it work.

We flew from Atlanta to New York to make our connection. The layover lasted three hours. While waiting, we talked with the Delta representative, who asked why Sandye was in a wheelchair. This one-of-a-kind agent had relatives who had MS as well, so her discussions were sincere and heartfelt. When the time came to board, the attendant said that she would board us first and take care of us. Then she found something wrong with the ticket and had to figure it out. We boarded early. The airport provided a handicapped aisle chair, which would take her to her seat. Three people tried to lift Sandye out, but I knew what to do and transferred her myself. If we had not boarded first, moving down the aisle with people seated would have been a nightmare. Usually, in public, she would have a urine bag strapped to her leg, hidden under her garments. She used a bed bag like one used in the hospital, on the plane due to the length of the flight and her not being able to get up to use the rest room. It took about ten minutes getting her set up while concealing her privacy issues. Just as the other passengers were boarding, the attendant came on board.

Attendant: "We have a problem."

Kent: "What's wrong?"

Attendant: "For some reason the flight was booked from Atlanta to New York, but the continuing flight was not paid for. You do not have a ticket on this flight."

Sandye was more worried about getting off the plane and exhausted. The look on her face was devastating.

Attendant: "Don't you worry, honey. I am going to fix this. You are going to take that dream birthday trip no matter what. I have got to work on this while the people board, but I'll be back."

We looked at each other with the knowledge that this trip was going to be very special. The thought of not taking this trip was like a bad dream. As the last people boarded, the attendant came back and said:

Attendant: "Now I must talk to you Kent. I have secured these seats as there is no way we are going to take her off the plane. I've got a specific person on the phone. When you land you need to call her and pay for these flights upon landing."

After all the trouble that we caused, I was in disbelief. I was sure that someone who had the tickets in first class had been bumped from their trip to Europe. As we flew away, we knew God was in control. First class was special with movies, steak, lobster, hot fudge sundaes and hot wet towels. We were pampered like royalty. We tried to stay awake to handle the jet lag.

We had a layover in Brussels, Belgium, before heading to Milan, Italy.

We learned through this adventure to always book direct flights whenever possible. The Air Italia flight held the next leg of the trip. Prior to boarding the plane, they announced that they had a problem. Our plane was not handicapped accessible. A new plane was needed. One of the pilots apologized and said they should have been prepared. We felt bad because we were holding up everyone else. Most onlookers have no idea how desperately handicapped people do not want to inconvenience others. A lift was used to board the new plane in the rear where food was brought on. The first class was small and separate from all the other seats. We were able to board first and were the only ones in first class. Sandye's body was exhausted but that was not going to stop her from enjoying every moment.

As we were flying over the Italian Alps, the snowcapped peaks were breathtaking. Flying over Lake Cuomo provided a scene that was spectacular with the mountains in the background. Sandye was leaning down in the seat, unable to see out the window. As I tried to straighten her up to see the sights, she grimaced in pain.

Sandye: "Please don't do that. It's not worth it."

It broke my heart that she could not enjoy this once in a lifetime view. At that moment, the pilot, who talked to us in the terminal, came out of the cockpit.

Pilot: "Isn't that view worth the wait?" (smiling at Sandye)

Sandye: "I'm so sorry that I can't see."

Pilot: 'We'll see about that."

Soon after his reentering the cockpit, to our astonishment, the plane dipped to the right so Sandye could get a full view of the mountains, the lake and the valley.

Sandye: "Wow! It's unbelievable."

I threw my arms around her and kissed her on the cheek as we experienced that moment together.

Kent: "I love you so much."

She smiled with a deep-felt unspeakable joy. The plane returned to a level flight. The pilot came out and spoke with his charming Italian accent.

Pilot: "What do you think of our mountains? Did you see them?"

Sandye: "Yes. I saw them. They were gorgeous. I can't thank you enough."

Pilot: "The people in the control tower do not like when I do that. I'll get my hands slapped for this one." (huge smile on his face)

We finally made it to Milan in one piece. Sandye's family was originally from Italy. Her mother was from the north near Venice while her father came from Sicily in the south. Before the trip, her father spoke on the phone.

Father: "You must go to in Milano." (spoken in Italian dialect)

"Milano," known as Milan, is in northern Italy. It is known as the business district and one of the great fashion cities of the world. On our way to the hotel, we noticed very small cars. A minivan was the biggest vehicle on the road. We arrived at a Marriott Renaissance hotel. Our plan was to be there for five days. The accessibility was not like the United States. The wheelchair would not fit between the bed and the wall. She was not able to walk and the door to the bathroom was also too small as well for the wheelchair to pass through. I went down to talk to the manager. This was their largest room. We had to make it work. I was about to do a lot of lifting and transferring, especially into the bathroom. This changed my respect level for what the United States has done to force companies to be handicapped accessible. No wonder we had not seen another person in a wheelchair there. This was a lesson for us to ensure that accessibility was assured on future trips. We were going to have fun, no matter what the obstacle.

The room had a large picture window that opened, allowing a breath of fresh air. A four-story apartment complex across the street held about twenty families. It was fascinating to watch their lifestyles. We stayed up after the flight to adjust for the six-hour time difference. I was exhausted, but Sandye was three times more. We went to bed at ten and woke up at seven.

Sandye: "What time is it?"

Kent: "Seven."

Sandye: "Morning or night?"

I went down to the lobby and found out that it was night. We had slept twelve hours more than we realized missing the whole first day, but she needed the sleep desperately.

The next day the first place we hoped to visit was a plaza in downtown Milan. We took a train. At the station we entered this huge plaza with people moving about everywhere. I looked to the left and couldn't believe what we saw. It was called the "Duomo di Milano." (magnificent church) We were in shock and stared intently at all the huge spires. Over a hundred covered the church and towered over the plaza. At the top of each spire was perched a statue of a saint.

Sandye: "Look Kent. There are people climbing on the roof.
I know that I can't go up there. I want you to go up there and
yell down."

As I entered the cathedral, I felt on hallowed ground. The magnificent organs, stained glass, and pews glistened by the light that shown through. The people spoke very little English. I climbed up carefully to the top and walked up the slanted roofs. I could see all of Milan and it was breathtaking ten stories up. I could see Sandye, as she was the only one in a wheelchair. I waved both arms until she finally saw me. She waved back. When I returned, we laughed with great joy about the experience. The hotel was about three miles away. We walked through the city with a lot of people due to the weekend. We headed through a park and heard a loud noise in the distance. Curiously, we headed towards the sound. It was singing and the closer we got, the clearer it was. At an amphitheater we saw at least a thousand children and teenagers. They were all dressed in the same uniform singing in Italian. We sat down and listened for some time. It sounded like the Vienna Boys Choir. We acted like these spur of the moment occasions were drawn up just for us. As we headed back to the hotel, we felt like they were serenading us through the city.

The hotel was a welcome sight to rest. One of the main reasons we left early was so that Sandye could get her strength back before Brenda and Robert arrived. It was a smart thing to do. Sandye spent the next two to three days resting and watching the families across the street. We did not want room service dinners every day, so, I went to an outdoor open-air restaurant, which were everywhere. In Europe, going out to eat was a whole night experience. You would pick fresh seafood sitting on ice from a cart that they would then cook for you. it was part of the dining experience. I tried to express to the owner that my wife was in a wheelchair, and I wanted an order to go.

Owner: "To Go. What is this TO GO?."

I explained the best I could, and he agreed to try and put a meal together for us. They wrapped the meal in paper and were not too happy about it. We loved the meal. It was fantastic. The next day I went back to thank the owner. As I turned the corner, he saw me and threw his hands up yelling.

Owner: "No TO GO. No TO GO."

I smiled and waved. Sandye and I laughed about it afterwards. What a contrast from America, where eating on the run is normal. We took a train on a day trip up into the Italian Alps. The trains in Italy are lovely experiences, passing little cottages, while enjoying expressos and chocolates. It was breathtakingly beautiful. The clouds covered the mountains, leaving us in a fog. We picked a town at random called Oulx to visit. There, we went to the first small restaurant with the windows open. It had a huge buffet of meats and cheeses. There were only ten people there with food for a hundred. The owner told us to help ourselves. All we wanted was a drink, but the food was free. As we enjoyed the sights, a motorcycle pulled up. An Italian man and an American lady began to share with us. She was from Connecticut and came over three months earlier. She met this man and stayed ever since. Italians were warm, passionate and inviting. They whisked away on the bike. We wondered what their life was like. It was amazing to see the Italian Alps up close and in person.

Our stay in Milan was winding down. We read in a magazine that Leonardo Davinci's mural painting of the Last Supper was in Milan. We decided to visit on our last day to see if we could get in. At a small church we saw a line of people who had booked tickets long in advance to see this masterpiece. Only twenty people could go in for ten minutes to view the painting. After about an hour we realized that we would not be able to get in. As we were taking pamphlets and about to leave, a tour guide saw us and invited us to join their group. The room we entered was temperature controlled to preserve the art. We couldn't believe what was happening. We learned that people are watching and are benevolent. We saw the original painting on a large wall. It was a spectacular moment to be relished forever. On the train the next day, we pondered what had filled our hearts.

The train took us across the north end of Italy towards Venice. We took a picture of the town of Verona two stops before Venice; yes, the Verona of Romeo and Juliet.

Sandye: "There it is. That's where my grandmother was born and where my mother's family is from. I'm sure we would see many relatives if we visited there. My father would be so happy."

We met two couples and shared experiences. They were well travelled. The sign of Venice led me to hurry to get the luggage off the train. The luggage was on the sidewalk before I realized that there were two Venice stops. This was not the one we wanted. The train began to move, while I reloaded the luggage in a panic. I threw the last suitcase on the moving train and jumped back on. Somehow, I was able to accomplish the task. I joined Sandye with the other guests we met.

Sandye: "There you are. We were wondering where you went. You're sweating. What's wrong with you?"

I could barely breathe and told them what happened. I was wondering what might have happened if the train left without me, carrying Sandye. We had to get off at the next stop and the others decided to help us. They knew that they only could carry one bag travelling in Europe. Four people hauled one bag of ours with their own. I don't know how we would have done this without their help.

Traveler: "Haven't you read Frohmer's book on travelling? You only take one bag." (sarcastic but also sympathetic to our cause)

Kent: "You got me there. I am so happy that you helped us."

There were no people available to assist travelers. We went directly from the train to small boats that held about twenty people. It was the only way to get to Venice. The only way I could get Sandye on to the boat was to carry her while the boat was rocking. As I stepped on the boat with her arms tightly around my neck, the boat shifted, throwing us towards the water. With all my strength, I managed to secure the boat and got her on board. One of her shoes slipped off into the water and sank.

Sandye: "At least I packed heavy with more shoes."

After the ride we had to walk a mile to our hotel with the four people adding our load of luggage to their own. Pigeons were landing on people in a beautiful plaza, called Saint Mark's Square, while five-piece orchestras were playing. Multiple churches were there, including the Saint Mark's Cathedral. Many movies used that sight in productions. Under my breath, I was cussing Margie for packing all that stuff in those suitcases. The four people were very gracious. The streets were very narrow without cars. We thanked our four new friends knowing that they were a life saver.. While we rested in our room, we meditated on all that had happened. Sandye's father had the Christmas tradition of giving and now we were on the receiving end. Four strangers went out of their way to help haul luggage for us all across Venice. It was a loving and charitable act of kindness that left an indelible mark on our lives. It seemed only fitting, that we would have that experience in Italy. In addition, we thought of the act of kindness by that flight attendant who ensured that we were able to make that trip. To this day, I wish I could meet her again.

Brenda and Robert were arriving the next day. The room was in a very small super expensive Best Western, but we got much needed rest. The next morning, we sat in a sidewalk cafe in Saint Mark's Square. The boats would drop off passengers in one area. From there, people would walk two blocks up a hill and down to the Square with their luggage. The café overlooked the sights, while we continued watching for Brenda and Robert. The tourists appeared weary as this was the only way they could enter the area. Gondoliers were bussing people in water taxis. This café became an experience in itself, watching people from all over the world peacefully yearning to come to this one plaza in Venice. The time had come and gone with no sign of Brenda and Robert. Five hours later, we decided to return to the hotel. There we received a message that they were detained for two more hours. We returned to the café to wait. We finally saw them pulling their bags trudging over the hill. I pushed Sandye in her wheelchair while shouting.

Kent: "Arrivederci. You arrived."

We had no idea it meant Farewell instead of hello and should have said ciao. Robert was so beat up and sweating. Brenda looked like she was worn out.

Brenda: "We are so happy to see you. I didn't think we could take any more. It was so hard to get here".

Sandye hugged Brenda and we went to the hotel. We enjoyed the Italian pizza and local fares, while we walked around the city with Sandye in her chair. The city was on an island. Four of us walking side by side up the very narrow streets would block a passageway. There were no cars in this area, only gondolier taxis to move you around. There is no place in the world like Venice, and it is worth a visit for the passionate experience. We boarded the Celebrity Cruise ship the next day, which was the same ship we took in Alaska. We knew where the handicapped room was in advance and reserved it at the rear of the ship. The room was eight stories up. From there we were higher than any building in Venice. It was like looking down from a cloud. The view was absolutely beautiful. The ship remained there for twenty-four hours so that sight was etched in our minds and hearts.

The room was huge with an extra-large back porch big enough to add a jacuzzi tub. With the four of us sitting there, I decided to give Sandye her birthday gift, though the actual date was not for four more days. I bought a diamond heart necklace. It was like Sandye, one of a kind. I told Sandye that my whole life was worth coming to this moment. Both Sandye and Brenda teared up, as I placed the necklace on her. Robert and I toasted. There was no place in the world we would have rather been than in Venice on this cruise ship with our friends.

The ship departed for Dubrovnick, Croatia the next day. While pulling up to dock we saw a beautiful old wooden bridge that reminded me of the Golden Gate Bridge but made with wood. It exuded a charm like no other for the thousand-year-old town that was in plain view from the ship. Someone told us to take a taxi to the top of the hill overlooking the bay, so we did that. At the top you could see bombed out houses from the Bosnia war. We walked out on a porch on one of the bombed abandoned homes and marveled at the sights of old Dubrovnick straight below us. To see such terror in such a godly place seemed ironic. We were experiencing something very special, unique and monique (too much) too.

After reboarding the ship, we headed for the Greek Islands. We arrived at Santorini the next morning. This time the cruise ship had to anchor in the water. That meant that we had to go down twenty steps then transfer onto a smaller boat to visit the island. There was no way Sandye was missing this island. The people working there were persistant and wanted to help carry her down the steps, but I knew how to maneuver the wheelchair forward backing them away. While tipping the wheelchair all the way back with Sandye staring face to face with me, I slowly let her down each step. Sandye had to trust me.

Sandye: "Don't let go of me."

Terrified Employee: "I have not seen this technique before."

I had to be very firm to keep her steady and avoid harming others. At the bottom of the stairs, they lifted her in the wheelchair onto the small boat. Sandye had her Greek aqua and white clothes on, which matched the country's colors. The beaches had black sand from the volcanoes. We had to then ride a gondola up to the town. We hailed a taxi to put the wheelchair in the trunk and Sandye in the vehicle. It was a lot of lifting but well worth it.

We had a nice meal overlooking the cliffs. All the houses were painted white, and the domes of the churches were aqua. There is nowhere else in the world like it. Brenda and Sandye were on cloud nine every moment. I bought a special gold Greek bracelet for Sandye sealing the moment and headed back to the gondola where Sandye and Brenda had a cocktail overlooking the ocean views. It was majestic.

Sandye and Brenda in Santorini, Greece 2007

Then we returned to the ship. As they lifted her to the small boat, they lost control and she fell, landing on her back on the floor of the boat. This hurt her. It was painful for her as we lifted her back into the wheelchair. I was upset for letting them take control when I knew better. This type of thing had happened before. At this moment I decided that no one and I mean no one would take control of the handicap situation unless I was in control. We know our partner's limitations and the best for them. Everyone's situation is different. We are the advocate for our loved ones and need to protect them every chance we get. After returning back to the room, I carefully got her in bed. Every inch of her was in pain. The next day was her birthday with a lot planned. The destination was Athens, Greece. Sandye took pain medicine but still had a rough night sleeping.

We had an excursion trip scheduled in Athens the next morning. I told Brenda and Robert to go without us as Sandye was unable to go. She stayed in bed until noon. The shipped was only docked that day in Athens from 7am to 6pm.

> Sandye: "This is my birthday. Our ship is leaving this port at six. Get me up. I am not missing Athens."

I worked up a sweat getting her ready as she sucked up the pain and moved forward. The ship docked at Athens, so we were able to exit directly to board a train. We hurried to get to the train as we knew we had not much time. The taxi drivers were hollering for us to go with them, but all I knew was to take a train. One taxi driver followed us a block down the street. He shouted:

> Taxi driver: "I know. I know." (pointing at the wheelchair)

I could see that this meant more to him than a taxi ride. While stopping and trying to make the right decisions, I felt something telling me to go with this gentleman even though he did not speak English. We put the wheelchair in his trunk and rode twenty minutes into the city. The driver drove fast and was excited that we were his passengers. His speed caused Sandy to yell, "WHOA, WHEE" like she was on an amusement ride. The driver was laughing. It was a wild ride. He took us to a store where one of his relatives spoke English. We learned that one of his other relatives was in a wheelchair. He knew what he had to do. His relative negotiated the deal for him to take us all over for the rest of the day. I told her that we did not bring a lot of money, but the driver was very sincere in wanting to help us. He said he would work it out.

He took us on bumpy roads to the Acropolis. Every bounce was painful,

Sandye was not going to miss anything. The Acropolis was one of the oldest buildings in the world. All tourists walked at least four hundred exhausting steps straight up to get to the building. He took us to the rear of the small mountain that held the building, where there was a special elevator built during the Para Olympics four years earlier. It took us to the top, where could see the historic monument without exhaustion. We were the only ones who did not look tired from the climb. He waited for us down at the cab and took us to an outdoor track, where the first Olympics was held. He then took us to a scenic overlook. There, I lifted Sandye up on a wall, pushed the wheelchair away and took a picture overlooking Athens and the Acropolis.

He then took us down a back road and had us get out. As we were sitting on the right side of a busy street, he drove his cab around the corner. We didn't know what to expect. He returned with a huge smile, while pointing at the ground and a building across the street. We waited five minutes. Then tourist busses pulled up with well over a hundred people. They got out of the busses and surrounded us.

Sandye: (smiling) "We must be in the right place."

At the top of the hour, bells started chiming. Doors on the right side of the building flew open. Armed guards dressed in kilts and furry hats marched out. There were six of them moving with their feet kicking high. It reminded us of Buckingham Palace and the changing of the guards or a scene from the Wizard of Oz. This event only occurred twice a day and we were right in the middle. We felt like we were seeing something that most on the ship had missed. In the taxi, the driver smiled back at us and giggled with a look like "I told you so." We both cheered for that man. I reached out, grabbed his hand and no words needed to be said. He felt my appreciation and joy, while I felt his sincerity and joy as well. He saved Sandye's birthday.

Back at the ship, the driver waited about forty-five minutes for me to take Sandye back up to the room and get her settled and return with the rest of his money. He was fine with that. The ship was about ready to leave and the only taxi that remained was with this man. When I gave him the money no words were spoken, only joy was in our faces. I grabbed his hand with both of my hands and it was obvious that this was a gift of love. Looking back, I can picture God choosing that driver to provide an unforgettable experience for us. At best, we could only have had time to see the sights from afar. The hundreds of steps would have taken their toll on both Sandye and I; not to mention the struggle we would have to return to the ship before it left. Sandye didn't miss anything and saw far more than she would have imagined. I thank God for that driver.

Brenda and Robert were supposed to join us that night for dinner and to celebrate Sandye's birthday, but Sandye was too tired. They were also tired from walking about ten hours, especially on those Acropolis steps. We covered everything in three hours and saw even more sights. We might have missed a meal, but those moments are cherished forever.

The next day and a half were spent at sea, giving Sandye time to recover. Our formal dining birthday experience was rescheduled. This is a chance for the guys to dress in tuxedoes and the girls to dress formally. Handicap situations require at least two hours extra time to help prepare. By the time she was ready with the medical issues, hair, and make up completed, I was running behind. Brenda and Robert came into the room dressed and ready. As she helped Sandye with the last item, Brenda saw that I was not properly attired.

Brenda: "Why aren't you dressed? Why didn't you dress

first?"

Kent: "Feel my shirt."

I was soaked in sweat from head to toe. Brenda conceded and took Sandye on the deck.

Brenda: "Go ahead and take your shower."

As we passed Sicily, we enjoyed cocktails. Brenda had bought a diamond Chanel necklace for Sandye and wore a matching one around her neck.

Brenda: "Now we are together wherever you go."

Both girls embraced and you could sense the love between them. *Celebrity* was known for their special dinners in the fine dining room. Even though it was after her birthday, all was well. God had the timing perfect. Robert and I enjoyed sharing drinks together as part of our bond. We docked later that night and awoke in Naples. Sandye's father was from there. Now we had come full circle. Robert went straight for the authentic pizza pie. While negotiating for a tour, we could sense the presence of a crime organization; they would not budge on the price. A private tour took us high with beautiful views of the cliffs and ocean.

The stay was short. The ship docked three hours from Rome the next day. We had to plan for a long day to tour Rome. Sandye looked up a private guide who picked us up at the ship. He was a bald man named, Fabio. He was very personable and spoke good English as he drove. He took us right to the Vatican. We were blown away by the sights. A huge line was in front, but Fabio took us to a special entrance in the back. They obviously knew Fabio. We went through a special entrance and avoided the crowds. Fabio stopped in a room.

Fabio: "This is the Pope's library."

Then he took us across the street to the Sistine Chapel.

Fabio: "Stay close. There're people everywhere."

We went inside and sat down in the middle of the floor. Fabio shared the history of the paintings (murals) on the ceiling. The employees were constantly hushing the crowds out of reverence. Fabio kept his voice low, but they never said a word to him. This is the place where they burn resin that gives off white smoke when a new pope is about to be announced. We were in awe! We then went to St. Peter's Cathedral, the largest in the world. The inside could hold about two football fields. While we were inside, a Catholic service was being held on the far end. Fabio guided us to a big marble statue called "The Pieta," by Michaelangelo. It depicted Jesus wounded and laying across his mother Mary's lap. Sandye sobbed.

Sandye: "Oh. My God."

I was moved in a way that I never felt before. Fabio then took us past the lover's stairs to a popular restaurant with a long line. After he talked to a gentleman, we were seated immediately.

Kent: "How did you find this guy?"

Sandye smiled, knowing that it was a coincidence. Someone was looking over her. While we ate a traditional Italian lunch, a man serenaded us with a saxophone. Fabio took us to the Trevi Fountain, where we could toss a coin over our shoulder for good luck. We went by the coliseum, where the Romans had men and animals battle. I would recommend spending a week in Rome, but what we did in five hours covered everything. I recommended Fabio to my boss, Pam, who went later and said it was the best part of her whole trip.

We were exhausted when we returned to the ship. Every day was packed, with Florence scheduled the next day. Our tour took us through beautiful wine country. Downtown Florence had twelve feet tall gold doors. Each door took the sculpture forty years to make. Within the door were Bible stories carved in gold. We were mesmerized by those doors and they also were worth the whole trip.

We were headed to another huge cathedral. In front of the third largest cathedral was a plaza with a restaurant. This was a large gathering area for people. The inside of the church was immense with statues, stained glass and other memories. People of notoriety were given burial plats beneath the church floors. We were in awe when Sandye tugged at my shirt.

Sandye: "We have a problem."

She had an accident and we needed a place to go to clean up. We went into a restaurant where no one spoke English. I led her back to the restroom, locked the door and saw a huge mess. I had back up clothes, but this would take a while. Because it took so long, the manager started banging on the door. Sandye urged me to speed up, while I shouted, "one minute." The manager repeated his banging after a minute. Sandye told me to just cut some of her clothes and toss them away. I finally finished while the manager still banged the door. We darted out of the restroom, with at least three people staring. Their eyes seemed to ask, "What have you been doing?"

I shouted "So sorry" as I ran out the door. Sandye told me that she would not want to be the person who used that restroom next. We laughed at the situation as it was way out of our control. Brenda and Robert knew not to ask questions. We then went across the street and viewed the Statue of David, which was remarkable. I learned that through perseverance, you will experience everything God has intended and more.

We stopped at the leaning Tower of Pisa the next day. Brenda and Robert went to Monaco while we stayed in Nice. We finished in Barcelona, Spain, where we had great local food in a wild party town and a incredible authentic dinner with sangria at local popular restaurant that was called the Siete Puertas; which meant the Seven Doors. Flying back through Paris, we took an Air France flight to Atlanta. Brenda sat next to Sandye. Robert and I sat behind them. The flight attendant came and told Sandye that they had a rule that her handicap required her to sit in a special seat in the middle of the cabin by itself. She was ready to have a great flight with her best friend in first class and this upset her. I stepped in and said that I could handle any emergency. This caused the plane to be delayed. The pilot said that we would be removed from the flight if she didn't move. I had no choice but to lift her into the new seat and spend as much time with her as I could. To keep Sandye from feeling isolated over the long flight, we all stood near her to keep her company. It was a real downer for such an incredible trip. Once we got home, we moved on and called it a trip of a lifetime. I told Margie that you need to read Frohmers and never pack like that again.

Just then the beeper went off on the IV Pole. The sound quickly brought me back to reality in the Hospital. I couldn't love her anymore while wondering what was to come, I prayed to God for her.

***

Chip, chip, chip. The artist desired new qualities in his work. God provides such joy on earth as a prelude to our future in heaven. Not only were the obstacles we faced overcome, but we experienced even greater blessings than we could ever imagine. God used others, like a taxi driver, a pilot, and strangers, to provide help and memorable moments. I learned to appreciate America for the work done to help the handicapped through the obstacles they faced. That trip was beyond anything we could have imagined. If heaven could out do that, we can't wait to get there. We also learned that we would have missed many wonderful blessings if we did not endure those trials along the way.

New Career Path

We needed to get a caregiver during the hours that I was away. Work was demanding. I had to travel on Mondays and return on Thursdays. This was stressful. Sandye could use the phone to reach me in an emergency. I put her to bed at ten at night and prepared enough meals for her and a caregiver. Then I would drive to my work destination late at night. To keep from falling asleep while driving I would call my friend Tracy in Houston. Her time zone was a little behind mine and she would help me pass the time many times over the years. I would get to the hotel around 2:00 in the morning which would allow me to make it to my appointment by 8:00 the next day. This was a brutal schedule. It was difficult to leave Sandye but we made it work.

We used the local newspaper to place an ad for a caregiver. A lady named Marion responded. She was a large lady who could also lift Sandye as needed in and out of her wheelchair. Marion was from Trinidad and Tobego, had a huge charismatic personality, (she looked exactly like Tyler Perry's Madea character) and Sandye loved that. On one of their first days out she used our handicapped van to take Sandye shopping, while I was still at home working. After a few hours, I started getting concerned. I called Marion's cellphone, and no one answered. Four hours later, I called the department store where they were headed and described the two women. I asked if anyone had seen them.

Store: "Oh, yes. They were here a few hours ago."

I really became worried after six hours and started calling the hospitals. No one had seen them. As I was about ready to leave to search for them, the van drove in the driveway. They left the van laughing and joking.

Kent: "Where have you been?"

Sandye: "We were shopping and then went to Johnny Rocket's. Everyone there began singing with us. Marion had a great time."

After realizing all the calls that I made, they knew that they needed to do a better job letting me know where they were. That would also help me give up control of protecting Sandye. We were comfortable with Marion. As long as Sandye was happy, so was I. I let Marion use the handicap van to drive back and forth from her home to our house when I was out of town. One time, I was out of state. The phone rang and Marion was all upset. While driving to a Shell station in the van, she hit the accelerator instead of the brake in front of the convenient store. The van struck and caved in the wall. She was ok but the van was totaled. No one in the store was injured, which was a blessing. Thank God Sandye was not in the van. My insurance went up dramatically, and I needed a new vehicle. Insurance companies use the Kelly Blue Book values but will not cover the handicap conversions. From then on that was the last time we let a caregiver use our vehicle for their personal use.

The Sugarloaf United Methodist Church small group became very close. One Sunday in the group, we mentioned our struggles with having my family over for the upcoming Thanksgiving. Fifteen people were coming. Most of them were guests. There was no way that we had enough time to prepare the house. Leroy and Linda, who headed the group, saw this as a great opportunity to bond.

Leroy: "I think we need to have a party at Kent and Sandye's home. When we are done, the house will be ready for their guests."

The following Saturday, twenty people converged at our home. Boxes, filled with Holiday decorations, were passed upstairs through a line of helpers. In addition, five bedrooms of furniture were filled from our basement storage. Food, fellowship, and laughter was the norm that day. When everyone was leaving, we were so grateful. Sandye's demeanor said it all and everyone knew our joy. This was the second small group of people from a church that became our close friends. I realized that church people love fun and as much or more fun than as my earlier social acquaintances. My previous stereotype was very wrong.

In 2008, Schwan's had a good sales year and decided to provide a trip for most of the salespeople to the Bahamas with their spouses. Management wanted me to bring Sandye, but it was getting much more difficult to travel. One of the other employee's spouses could not come on the trip, so she offered to give up her ticket for our caregiver to go as well. Marion was born and raised in the islands and was very happy to go back. Travelling was hard on Sandye's body, but she wanted to do that for me! We stayed in a room with an ocean view, while Marion's room was next door. We enjoyed sightseeing while many enjoyed the various water sports. Everyone dressed formally at the awards dinner. Marion came two hours early realizing the difficulty in dressing Sandye, while she laid on the bed. We got her ready in time. Marion stayed in her room, while Sandye and I made the dinner with about two-hundred-fifty people.

It frustrated Sandye when I had to help her eat, especially in front of people that we knew. Loading her fork with food was no longer a simple task. She started to avoid those situations. It was unavoidable. My boss and others would see me feeding her. We ignored it and tried to have a good time. Awards were distributed after the dinner. They went through a lot of awards without acknowledging me. Sandye knew that I had a good sales year.

Sandye: "Why haven't they called your name?" (whispering)

Kent: "I'm not sure, but I may be winning the big award."

Sandye: "Two things you need to be aware of. First, don't cry. Then make sure your zipper is up."

The award was for the national sales for food service for Schwan's. I won that award and made good on half of her suggestions. My zipper was up. We made it back home, although Sandye struggled. What a blessing in that she wanted to do that for me! Flying was no longer an option in the future. Two months later I saw a three-page article called, "Riding with the national Sales Champion," that was written by a Schwans company reporter who spent a day with me. I was deeply moved.

Valentine's Day was nearing. I had purchased several pictures from a local artist to give to Sandye and was on my way to obtain one more. This artist was known for combining spiritual context to Christmas scenes. The drive took over an hour. On the drive back, Marion called.

Marion: "Come home quick. Sandye is not looking good."

I hurried home and went into the room to see Sandye.

Marion: "Kent, look at her foot."

Sandye would accidentally bump her toes while maneuvering the wheel-chair and not feel it, due to the numbness from her MS. Her big toe appeared infected. Her foot was swollen and discolored. Her communication was also distorted. I knew that I needed to rush her to the hospital. They admitted her shortly after we arrived. The nurse put a magic marker line up her foot to her ankle marking how far the infection had travelled from her toe up her ankle.

Nurse: "You're going to be here for a few days."

Sandye: "Well, you better hurry. We have plans for a very fine Valentine's dinner at a French restaurant."

Nurse: "You are going to miss that dinner."

The following day, after being admitted, a new line was drawn halfway up her leg.

Nurse: "If this line gets pass your knee, you may lose your leg."

After two days, the antibiotics started to work, and the infection receded back down her leg. I knew that she was happy about that but brokenhearted about missing the planned Valentine's dinner. One afternoon, while she was in the hospital asleep, I dressed up in suit, turned on music and waited for her to open her eyes.

Kent: "Welcome to our Valentine's date. Madame, would you like to dance to the next song?"

Sandye: Smiling but still a bit groggy. "Yes sir. I would love to."

I held her close and rocked back and forth to a beautiful song. At the end of the song, I went to the closet and retrieved the new artist's picture.

Sandye: "Oh Kent. When did you have time to get that? You shouldn't have."

Men should know that they always SHOULD HAVE.

***

Chip, chip, chip. The masterpiece begins to take on an explosion of detail that comes from heartfelt giving. Trusting God, and the abilities He has given me, is reaping rewards. Balancing work and caregiving can be difficult without trust and faith. Setbacks are often opportunities for God to work. Gifts given from the heart provide the best reactions. Being receptive to receiving help from others is crucial, especially from people who sincerely care about us. This helps to maintain balance and sanity during volatile situations.

Heart for Giving

Sponsoring families over the holidays like we did in Dallas was still heavy on our hearts. Giving to others started replacing the dreams of traveling, which felt really good. We started looking for opportunities from the church to minister. That worked well for a couple of years. Then we heard a Christian radio station instituting a Chick Fil-A giveaway program at Christmas. That excited us, because it sounded like the Dallas program. We met the live broadcast at the local restaurant near us. About fifteen binders contained wishes and needs for us to scan. We located a family where a fireman, we will call Joe, his wife and two children had wishes presented by another fireman, we will call Bill. Joe was injured in a fire where his partner, we will call Bob, was killed.

Bill wrote passionately about his injured friend and coworker. This seemed like a much bigger task than the ones we did in Dallas, but the need was so big we couldn't pass it up. We called Bill to see if we could surprise the family. After a great conversation about Joe and Bob, he said that Bob played the bagpipes. Joe wanted to learn how to play the bagpipes as a tribute to Bob's life. This was a job for Sandye.

She called all over the city to find someone who would teach Joe how to play the pipes. After a few days searching, a lady was located. Sandye shared the story and the lady was so moved that she donated six months of lessons. In addition, the family was in need, so we decided to give gift cards. We purchased a spa package for Joe's wife. We planned to meet Bill at the home of the receiving family. The wife was contacted to ensure they would be home.

Bill brought two more firemen with him, which surprised Joe. We explained that Bill had submitted a wish for Joe and his family and knew how important the bagpipes were to both he and Bob. After giving the gift cards and the spa for the family, we shared that we found someone who wanted to teach Joe to play the bagpipes for six months; so he could play for his fallen brother. This was too much for him to take in. As the tough fireman that he was, he left to go outside. He did not want to breakdown in front of his wife. The other three firemen followed as we hugged his wife.

> Wife: "You don't know how much this means to our family. I cannot express it in words. (tears running down her face) We will remember this forever and it will help my husband heal."

We left feeling a warm sense of gratification that is indescribable in words. This feeling was incredible and I couldn't wait to give more.

The Schwan company asked me to tour a plant in Kentucky where pizzas were made. We were between caregivers. Marion had moved on. I called an agency that would send caregivers to help. The problem was that we couldn't always get the same person. A few we liked, but there was no guarantee. My phone rang while at the pizza plant near the ovens. I could see it was Sandye who would never call me at work unless it was an emergency. I excused myself, though it was uncomfortable.

> Sandye: "KENT." (screaming over the machine sounds)

I hurried over to a quiet place while she kept screaming my name.

Kent: "What's wrong?"

Sandye: "I just woke up from a deep sleep and there is a large dark man at the end of the bed."

Kent: "What? (knowing that the agency would never send a man) Who is it?"

Sandye: "He says he is from the agency. (voice still trembling) I told him to leave the room, because I was in a nightie and helpless."

Kent: "Where is he now?"

Sandye: "He's in the hallway or the kitchen. He's still in the house."

Kent: "Let me call the agency and I'll call you right back."

When I got the agency's owner, she said that she knew we preferred females but no one else was available. I was furious because that came without warning and when I was not home. I called Sandye back and asked her what she wanted to do. She said she was not comfortable. I called the agency back and insisted that the man leave. Then I called a friend who could help until I returned from my trip. I hung up shaking helplessly. When I caught up to the group, they asked "Where have you been?" I replied, "Don't even ask." When I arrived home, I couldn't wait to comfort

Sandye. We knew we needed a permanent caregiver.

This was a tough time physically for both Sandye and I. It was starting to take a toll. She needed to transfer from the bed to the chair, then the chair to the car, then the car back to the chair and so on. There were times when I would have to lift her twenty times in a day. She could help some. As time wore on it was getting to be more of a dead lift. One day I felt something pop in my stomach and there was now a bulge coming out of my belly button. I now had a hernia that needed surgery. It wasn't a major surgery but the doctor told me that I would only have eighty percent usage and if I ever reinjured it I would lose more ability. So I had to be careful. It took three months before I could lift her again and she was forced to use the Hoyer lift with the caregivers. From then on, I had used a weight belt and been careful not to reinjure my body. I have learned that if you don't take care of yourself, you cannot take care of others. It must be a priority.

In the first year in the home, we had the basement finished as a place for a caregiver to stay. Someone recommended a special education teacher named Lacey and her son J.B. as a tenant for our downstairs apartment. J.B. was five years old with cerebral palsy. He needed total care. Before they could move in, we installed a sidewalk to the downstairs. When the cement was nearly dry, we asked Lacey if we could imprint her son's hand in the cement as a reminder and tribute. We discounted the rent to further assist Lacey's needs. They were the cutest family and perfect for our basement. We became close with her and helped when J.B. needed something.

We just purchased a used handicap van for ourselves. Lacey had to lift J.B. into their standard minivan. A new handicapped van cost between sixty and seventy thousand dollars properly equipped. We decided the need for handicap equipped vans was so high and people could not afford them, that we would focus our giving on helping people get them. We purchased three vans at discount prices and resold them for three thousand dollars profit each. When we reached nine thousand dollars, we were able to purchase an old equipped converted handicap van and then give it away to a needy family. Lacey's friend, who drove the handicapped bus, adopted a teenage girl with a handicap. They were in desperate need of quality transportation, as the girl was too big to get in a car. After school, we gave them the van. They wanted to meet Sandye. They were blown away by this gift. All we wished for was a picture of them and sent them to remember this sweet moment. We then wished them well and sent them on their way, knowing their quality of life would be better.

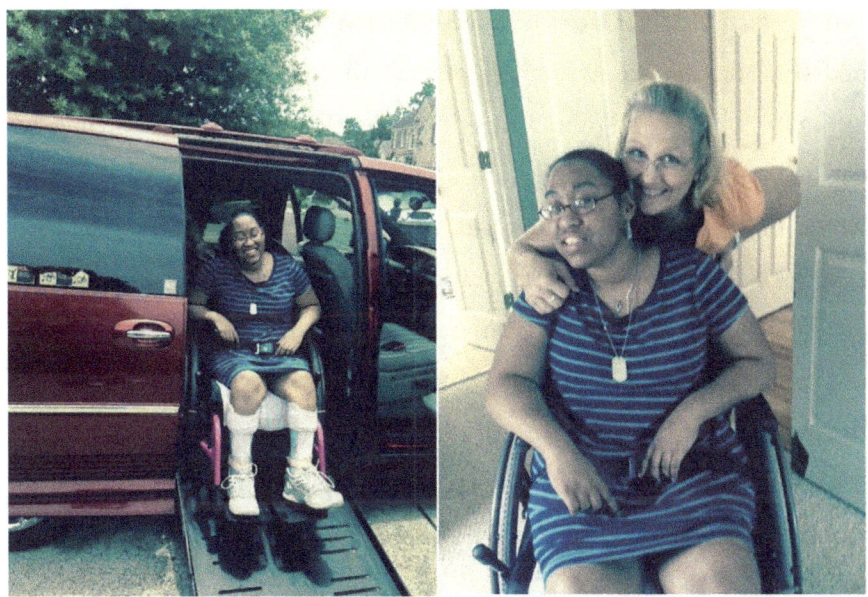

First van giveaway (mother and daughter)

Our six months of buying vans and selling built up to this moment and we felt exhilarated. This left a desire to do more. On every trip I kept my eyes open for other vans. Florida provided many opportunities for van purchases, which I would buy and drive back.

We had a business trip opportunity that would include pleasure in Ashville, N.C. Sandye joined me on this trip but liked to keep our personal life and business separate. We went to the Grove Park Inn to host customers. One of our Vice Presidents was there, so I had to be on my best behavior. The room was not ready, so we found our way into a ball room. They were filming a cooking contest for the Food Show Network. It was a contest for four different chefs to make a Christmas display. Sandye absolutely loved it. Our room was available four hours later, but Sandye stayed in the ballroom an additional four hours in awe. The host of the show interviewed Sandye and gave her an autographed apron, which Sandye gave to Brenda. Brenda loved that TV show.

The rest of the planned events and dinners became very difficult for Sandye to attend. Her face told a story of deep concern and these trips were not worth it anymore. When we got back home, we were down. We knew we had to change from our trips of the past. A couple of days later, we decided to pivot by having vacations at home in the future. This way we would have her friends come to us, so she would not miss the joy of the experience. It would now be staycations of joy!

The pressure was on me from Schwan's management to travel three nights per week. I made it clear that I needed to move to another area of the company or leave. Sandye and I were constantly praying for relief. Out of the blue, I received a phone call from the regional manager from Foster Farms, who accepted the job that I turned down ten years earlier. His name is Gene.

Gene: "Kent, are you interested in coming to work for Foster Farms?"

Kent: "You've got to be kidding me. I turned down the offer ten years ago. Why would they be interested in me now?"

Gene: "That doesn't matter if you're the right person. My

position is open as I am moving to a new location in the company."

The next thing I knew is that I was on my way to interview with them. On the plane I shared this story with the lady sitting next to me on the plane. She was a Christian comedian and shared how God works things like this out. She had written several books and later sent some to me. When we exited the plane in Los Angeles, the lady asked me if it was ok for her to pray for this job in the middle of the terminal. I didn't care and she prayed in a loud roar for God's will, while holding her hand on my shoulder. It was amazing to feel free while someone prayed, even with people moving all around us. We hugged and I went on to my San Francisco connection for the interview. There, I interviewed with seven people and three were the same ones there ten years earlier. I got the job.

This position covered the southeast. It was a family-owned business that allowed employees to do whatever they needed to do to handle business, which was exactly what we needed at the time. Sandye and I breathed easier as the pressure for weekly multiday travel was lifted off our shoulders.

Administrative people helped me through those areas that were out of my comfort zone, like paperwork. Neta Pombo was the person at Foster Farms that gave me that assistance. She was more than willing as she saw that I would fall behind with my paperwork. While driving in the handicap van to the airport to pick up Margie, Neta talked to me over the speaker phone. Sandye, who was very excited to see her friend, was sitting in her wheelchair behind the front seat; while steadying herself using the backseat handles. It just finished raining and steam was rising off the hot pavement. At seventy-five miles an hour, the car ahead did not see the traffic had come to a complete stop. The car hit a minivan without braking. The minivan went airborne, turned sideways, and the vehicle struck slid below. Every car slammed on the brakes simultaneously. When I hit the brakes hard, my phone slipped down onto the footwell of the passenger seat. Cars on both sides tried to stop, leaving nowhere for me to go. I came within two feet from hitting the smashed vehicle. The cars on both sides of us started a chain reaction of accidents. I could see a large semitruck in the rear-view mirror bearing down behind us with brakes locked. We cringed and waited for the impact that never happened. After every car stopped, eight cars were wrecked in front of us and on both sides. Our car and the truck behind us were the only ones spared.

I thought about the fact that Sandye did not go through the windshield. She had held on to the back seat with white knuckles. If she had not done that, she would have been severely hurt. It was a miracle that we were untouched. The semi would have destroyed us. As we later pulled away from the accident, unharmed, I retrieved my phone and called Neta back.

Neta: "Oh my God. I heard that whole accident. SLAM, BANG, SMASH, ...Are you OK?"

Kent: "You are not going to believe this, but God protected us completely."

This was amazing timing, because Neta was a professed agnostic. We had a close relationship, and this made us even closer.

***

Chip, chip, chip. The artist used others to help with the work. Just as God has placed people in our lives to help us, He has also opened our eyes to see the needs of those around us. I have learned servanthood and great joy as a result. As Sandye's disease continues to decline, the stress between work, caregiving, and vacations increases. God provided a new direction and huge relief. God showed us how to reinvent new directions to find joy through the journey. Oh, how my faith has grown, and my heart rejoices. God showed me that He was protecting us in a miraculous way.

Joy with Friends

My friend from Schwan's, who I used to talk with on late nights while driving, was Tracy Desmit. She had the same position covering Texas that I did in the Southeast. She was extremely successful and had won numerous awards. We became good friends. She was so compassionate towards Sandye and me. When I left Schwan's, a position opened in Texas with Foster Farms. I was able to get Tracy employed a year later. Our ongoing friendship remains to this day. Neta was our inside salesperson and common link for both of us. We were a good team and getting close personally in addition to work pals. Some people called Tracy my "work wife" which Sandye thought was hilarious.

Knowing that Sandye would have a tough time meeting new friends, it was crucial that she stay in touch with Brenda and Margie. The money that we would normally spend on travelling was now available to fly her friends in for visits. This was the case for Margie. On the way back from the airport, it was dark outside, and Sandye had turned her wheelchair facing back towards Margie. They were talking and laughing. I made a sudden stop hitting the brakes hard, which threw Margie on the floor in front of Sandye. Sandye yelled at me, while reaching out in the dark space to find her friend.

Sandye: "Kent! Margie flew on the floor. (While waving frantically) Margie, Margie!"

Margie: "I'm down here. (laughing hysterically in the dark) That will teach me to fasten my seatbelt."

Both girls started laughing, knowing they were both OK. I shook my head wondering what was coming next. Their time together was special. I realized that the more I treated them with meals and special events, the more enjoyment all of us felt. While back at our house, Margie and Sandye were playing in the living room. Sandye had her new electric wheelchair. The old electric wheelchair was still in our possession. Margie decided to test drive the old chair. The tires made a circular pattern around the living room and kitchen. Sandye thought she was Mario Andretti, lowering her head chasing Margie. Margie was screaming with excitement as Sandye would catch up to her. The path that they were taking was like a lap at the speedway. The walls were struck repeatedly causing holes. The girls were laughing so hard that I didn't care about the damage. I would fix it all later. Their joy was worth every minute I spent plastering.

The commute to our old church in Sugarloaf was forty minutes one way. We loved the pastor there and our small group. Suddenly one Sunday, our pastor read a letter of immediate resignation with no reason. With two-thousand members, this church was one of the fastest growing Methodist churches in the country. This news sent the whole congregation into a tailspin. I realized that people in his position are just as human as the rest of us. In the past I had put people on pedestals. We all put our pants on in the same manner. Leroy, our small group leader, had a massive heart attack and passed away shorty after. Over the next few months our small group began to break up. We knew that we had to find a church closer to our home. We bounced around looking for the right fit, not knowing how long it would take. With Sandye's big obstacle of MS, smaller changes surprised us.

On another occasion, Margie was helping Sandye in the bathroom, while I was away. Sandye's urine bag needed to be emptied into a container. Sandye would only let caregivers or me do this job. It was important for her friends to not be her caregivers, but Margie was different. She had a way with making everyone feel at ease in tough or awkward situations. As Margie started to help, the urine bag popped loose.

> Sandye: "Oh no! I knew it." (not wanting her friend to be in this mess)

> Margie: (sensing Sandye's frustration) "Don't worry. I got it."

Pee was going everywhere. Both girls were covered.

> Margie: "Now, I got a golden shower."

> Sandye: "Oh! You better put some gloves on."

> Margie: (looking up) "Sandye, that ship has sailed."

It was another difficult situation where both girls laughed hysterically. I knew that I had to bring Margie back as much as possible in the future. Friends, acting as caregivers in hard situations, made a huge difference. Margie was one of those special people.

Sandye and her dear friend Margie

We were trying to locate the right caregiver. Companies that offered that service were not consistent. We placed a personal ad in the local paper. A lady named Kerry Smith applied for the job. She was separated from her husband with two children. She had a great personality. The job required personal strength to lift Sandye in and out of her wheelchair. Sandye did not want to use the mechanical lift as it made her feel debilitated. She seemed like a great fit with Sandye as both enjoyed devotionals. She loved reading the book, "Jesus Calling."

Sandye's nerves at this time were really flaring up and would cause a burning sensation. It made her feel like snakes were crawling on her. She would look down on her legs and ask me to remove the snakes. I would see nothing, but she insisted. I went through the motions anyway to give her a sense of relief. It got so bad one day, when I was out of town, that Sandye asked Kerry to take her to the psychiatric hospital due to extreme pain. The doctor at the hospital asked if she could see the snake. She always responded negatively, but she could feel it. They could not help her because it was a nerve feeling and not a psychological event. She needed to go to a neurologist. When I returned from my business trip, Sandye and Kerry had made notecards with scriptures addressing pain. These were placed throughout the house. Whenever Sandye felt discomfort, she would read the cards for relief. Many of these cards remained until we moved years later.

Dr. Stuart was her MS neurologist. Sandye cried out in his office that he needed to give her something for relief. He prescribed a drug called, Lyrica. It helped somewhat but had bad side effects. Her feet swelled up and turned purple. She went from a size eight to eleven. On her next visit to Dr. Stuart, she wondered what other patients did for help.

> Dr. Stuart: "Not all my patients have this experience. Those that do, have the same experiences as you. We have no treatment. They learn to block it out." (Sad look)

Sandye had a look that cried, "You have got to be kidding me." He sent us to a few other specialists, trying other medication without success. After all options were tried, we were driving home heartbroken. I could see that she wanted to give up. I helped her in bed. I made the decision to leave a whole bottle of pain pills for her to take when she needed them. I left the house and drove around crying out to God in agony and feared that she might try to take her life. When I got back home, Sandye was awake in the bedroom.

> Kent: "Sandye, I thought you were going to take all of those pills and end the misery." (tears running down my face)

> Sandye: "Are you kidding. I would never give up my chance

to be with Jesus. Taking my life would jeopardize that."

I knew that we were in this for the long haul and could get through anything with God's help and each other.

Dr. Stuart prescribed a Marinol pill (Marijuana) that helped her internally.

> Kent: "Doctor, what do you think about the other forms of Marijauana? Do you think they would help with the nerve pain? I have heard that they have helped people with MS."

> Dr. Stuart: "I am not opposed to you finding anything that will work, I have exhausted all medical options. But make sure you find a source that you trust."

I went on the search to find this drug that would help. When we returned three months later.

> Kent: "We found some Marijuana to help Sandye."

> Dr. Stuart: "What did you find?"

> Kent: "Well, there is one pill that you prescribe and then there is a liquid form that take in drops, or the regular weed that you smoke."

> Dr. Stuart: "Which one did you purchase?"

Kent: "All of them."

Dr. Stuart: "Who did you get them from?"

Kent: "A man in my Bible study group."

Snickering Dr. Stuart: "Well, there you have it."

Sandye smiled knowing that Dr. Stuart would do anything to help relieve her pain and now this medicine, when used the correct way, helped her survive.

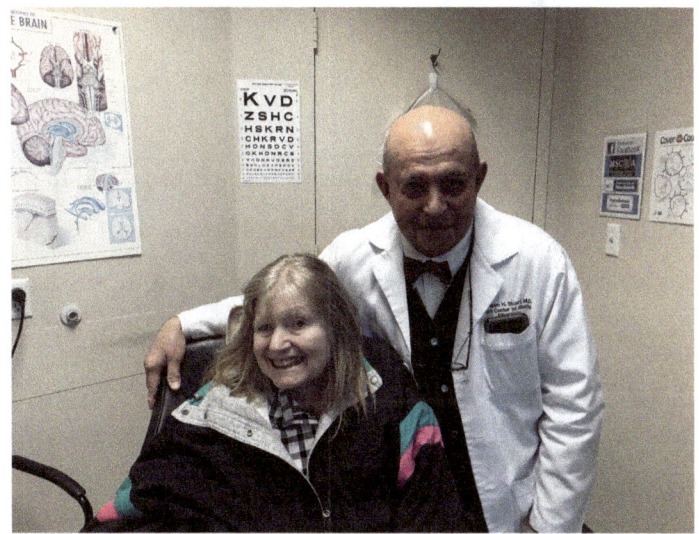

Sandye and Dr. Stuart during routine visit in Atlanta

Kent and Dr. Stuart at nonprofit
golf fund raiser for MS Center of
Atlanta

I thought about going in front of the government to plead to nationally legalize marijuana for people like Sandye that had no other recourse.

Because Sandye's health was failing, we decided to invite friends and neighbors to a toga party at our house for my fiftieth birthday party. The only rule was that all guests had to wear some sort of Toga outfit. If you didn't show up with one, we had one for you. Prior to big events, Sandye's nerves would act up. We cancelled about half of the previous activities that we committed to. For this event, our neighbor Susan helped dress Sandye in a pink satin outfit. When she was finished, Sandye looked like a Greek goddess, with makeup and beads in her hair. Sandye pushed through all the pain to make my day very special.

My old boss Pam and her husband came in GI Joe camouflaged toga outfits. Brenda and Robert drove up from Florida. Robert's toga outfit closely resembled Fred Flintstone. Russ did not like to dress up, but his wife Leslie did the minimum to help him participate. A chef friend named Kami, who worked at Schwan's, graciously catered the event. The theme for the food was Greek and delicious. About thirty people were there, all in toga attire. Music was blasting from "Animal House." Because Sandye tried so hard, I had a great time. Near the end, Kami came to me with disturbing news. Robert had been making a pass towards her and she felt that she had to leave the party early. I could see that Robert had an alcohol problem. Sandye continued to stay close to Brenda over the next few months as she could see that Brenda and Robert's relationship was in trouble. Sometimes God shows us that MS is not the only problem He sees. Except for that issue, everyone in attendance thoroughly enjoyed the party. It was a memorable time.

Just when I thought as we were leveling out to an even keel, as we were heading home from the local CVS drug store, Sandye's wheelchair was loaded into the van. The trip was less than a mile from our home, so I decided to not strap the chair down. Turning the corner sharply onto the main road caused her chair to flip to the right. She landed on her head with the wheelchair on top of her. She screamed in pain. Freaking out, I pulled off the road and put the van in park. I leaped to pull the chair off her. Then I realized that the car was in reverse; backing into the street and doomed to be in a bad collision with ongoing traffic. Reluctantly, I had to lay her back down on her neck to stop the van from colliding with oncoming vehicles. She continued screaming. I thought I broke her neck. Once the van was secured in park, I was able to get the wheelchair back up with Sandye in it. I was certain that she was severely hurt by the fall and weight of the wheelchair. Although shaken and sore, she was OK. I learned a valuable lesson that day. Always take the safety precautions, no matter how far the travel, and strap the wheelchair down at all times. I beat myself up for a long time for hurting her again, but like the Timex watch, Sandye took a licking and kept on ticking.

***

Chip, chip, chip... The work takes on spiritual qualities. Great friends and caregivers provide help in times of need as well as joy. Sandye's faith provides the strength she needs to overcome difficult times. It also lifts my spirits when I am troubled. My shortcomings may have put Sandye in harm's way at times, but God is in control.

Caregivers

Kerry was a professional caregiver but needed personal help. She had to separate from an unhealthy personal relationship and remove her two daughters. The father had legal issues that would affect the children's safety. Our basement apartment was available, so we let them have it on moment's notice. We loved her children and thought it was a good match. They moved in one evening. The next morning, I came out onto my deck and looked down outside the apartment. I saw Kerry's boyfriend holding his child like he was moving in with them. Alarm bells went off, knowing this man's background. Now, our household was in harm's way as I feared for Sandye. I called Kerry upstairs after she was alone to talk. I told her that the boyfriend was not allowed there, and if he came around, she could not stay in our home. The man had a checkered past. He was in trouble with the police. I could not jeopardize my wife and bring that risk into my home. The man agreed to not return and Kerry was able to stay there.

Kerry was our caregiver for about a year and a half. Even after we hired a new caregiver, Kerry lived downstairs for another three months. The next two years were volatile in trying to get the right care for Sandye. We loved and missed Kerry, she was right there for Sandye while dealing with some of the worst symptoms that she had in her lifetime. We learned a valuable lesson. We all have baggage, including caregivers and must be mentally prepared. Our desire to help others also includes discernment.

Lacey lived with her son JB, who had cerebral palsy. She reached out to us for new living quarters. She used to live in our basement, but now it was occupied. We opened our upstairs for her to live with us. JB was now ten years old. That provided new opportunities for sharing. This arrangement would be difficult due to JB's twenty-four-seven needs along with Sandye's struggles. Lacey was also a special education teacher who took JB with her to school every day. I started to take on a parental role with JB, helping him climb the stairs each night before bed. As he lifted each leg, we could hear Sandye singing.

Sandye: "One foot, one foot, one foot in front of the other."

As she sang, JB smiled and worked harder to climb the stairs. This became a daily tradition. Over time, we built a very close bond with Lacey and her son. We attended his T-ball games and screamed for him to run to first base or drive his wheelchair. One Halloween we put JB in a wheelchair that would raise him up to a vertical position. He had great fun screaming as trick or treaters came to the door, which actually scared them. Sandye could hear him laughing and shared in his joy.

Lacey and JB while living in our home

The need for caregivers became even more important. Sandye was struggling physically and would often go into deep sleeps. This allowed caregivers to have free rein in the house. The latest caregiver took exception to how she felt treated. I was concerned for Sandye's safety, but the caregiver's personal life took a back seat. The caregiver was late one day and I responded negatively. A neighbor of hers had a problem that caused her delay. She responded with anger that we didn't care for her own well-being or her neighbors. You could feel the tension and we had to part ways. Her attitude seemed to tell us that something was not right.

We then searched for another caregiver. We placed an internet ad and a lady, named Renae, came to our door. I was concerned that she would not handle the physical needs for Sandye. She seemed quiet and completely opposite of the caregivers from the past. I had to force the conversation.

Kent: "Why are you here?"

Renae: "I really need a job right now."

Kent: "Can you tell us something about yourself?"

Renae: "My husband flipped his car a month ago and died."

There was an uneasy silence afterwards. I saw Sandye's eyes and knew that we had to give her a chance. It was so tragic.

Kent: "How are you able to have the strength to come here today?"

Renae: "I rode the bus back from North Carolina and knew that I had to do something. I prayed and saw your ad online and knew it was for me."

Kent: "We are not using equipment to transfer Sandye. So, like all the caregivers we hire, if you can physically handle and transfer Sandye in the bedroom, you are hired."

I wanted to see if Renae could roll Sandye over using the sheet. She pulled hard and Sandye flipped over with ease like a pancake.

Kent: "Wow! You're strong."

Renae: "I used to be a weightlifter."

She was always trustworthy and on time. God knew exactly what he was doing with Renae and her future husband Kendrick to our home.

She proved to be specifically what Sandye needed in crucial life-threatening times. Sandye and Renae became very good forever friends.

Sandye with her special friend/caregiver Renae (Rakesha Blue)

***

Chip, chip, chip... The work appears to have strong support. God provides help for those in need and uses us as caregivers. Just as Renae served to provide for Sandye's needs, Sandye's singing was an encouragement to JB. With God we are never alone.

Faith and Giving

We started to intensify our van mission projects. All the previous energy that we spent to save, plan, and go on trips in the past was now focused on helping people with handicapped vans. Its as if God filled a missed joy of traveling with a joy of giving, and it was more fullfiling. I would look for handicapped vans on each trip to the southeast.. This was a lot of work but very therapeutic. Those who sold the vans would share their stories. Knowing that these vans would serve others like it had done for them was joyous. We sold those converted vans to others in need. After their loved one had passed, they would contact me to repurchase the van at little or no cost for others.

Over a period of three or four years, we were able to purchase twelve vans, which afforded us to give away four with the profits. There was no better feeling that we received, than giving a van to someone in need, knowing that it would change their life. This giving helped our love for one another bond our love to grow closer together.

Taking a shower was difficult for Sandye. She needed the right chair to support her. I took a plastic outdoor patio chair and placed it in the shower. I lifted her from her wheelchair over the thresholds of the shower onto the patio chair. Which was a tough lift on my back. She enjoyed feeling the warm water. I had to leave for a few minutes to go to the bank. When I returned, Sandye was laying on her back covering the drain. The water pooled up, causing her to shiver from the cold. It scared me half to death. I couldn't believe I left her. I restored the chair and lifted her back on it. I started the warm water again. I didn't realize that the chair had cracked. As I turned my back, she flipped and fell again, cracking her head on the floor. In desperation, anger flowed through my body. I screamed while slamming the wall with my open palm. I screamed out of guilt and anger for my wife. I put her in bed and she survived for another day. I knew that I would never leave her again in situations like this and sometimes I just could not control the outcome.

For two years we searched other churches to find a new church. We were briefly attending a United Methodist church where Sandye did not feel spiritually fed. While leaving the church Sandye, a bit frustrated, asked if we could just go for a drive. We came to a stop sign.

Sandye: "Pull into that parking area right there!"

I pulled up to a small church not too far from our house, which Sandye had pointed out before.

Sandye: "Go in and find the pastor."

I entered the worship center and noticed that the service had just concluded. I asked one of the sound technicians about the pastor and he pointed the man out. I waited until he was free.

Kent: "Pastor."

Pastor: "Please call me Dustin."

Kent: "My wife and I would like to meet you. She had a strong feeling to come to this church. She has MS and is resting in the van in the parking lot. Do you have a minute to speak to us."

Dustin: "Absolutely!" (with a gleam in his eye)

He excused himself from others and made his way to our van. I opened the side door of the van with Sandye in her wheelchair secured to the floor.

Dustin: "Hello there. It's very nice to meet you. My name is Dustin."

Sandye felt a comfort and smiled.

Dustin: "Can I give you a hug?"

Sandye: 'Sure, I would love that."

I knew there was something special happening. We talked for an hour and felt comfortable in knowing that we found a new place to visit and hopefully call home. Dustin had a disposition that was soothing. We attended the next Sunday. Inside the church foyer was a picture on the wall.

Sandye: "Hey, Kent. I cannot believe that they have the same Thomas Kincaid picture of Jesus that we have in our house."

We knew that something special was there. We have not seen that picture anywhere else before or after. Often, we would arrive early and pray with music playing. Soon, the Cornerstone Church started a small group ministry. Dustin asked us if we would be willing to host a group in our home. A couple, Larry and Polly, came to our home and said that they would be the group leaders. He was in the food business as well. Polly was a professor of a local college. We bonded very quickly with them. The group began with five couples and met every Sunday after church. On those occasions when we could not attend church, the small group would come to us. We came to find out much later that this church was affiliated with the Asseblies of God. We never cared what denomination a church was as long as they were following and loving like Jesus.

Food was part of the fellowship every week. One Sunday we brought out all of our crazy hats. We took a picture with the initial eight people in the group wearing the funniest hats ever. I realized that I was having as much fun with them as I had with my drinking buddies. The thought of Christians being dull was only a myth, plus it did not come with a hangover. The realization that our life seemed to be on an even keel when we were engaged in small groups became special. Some other people from the church heard about the fun and fellowship. The group doubled in size in just a couple of months. Our motto was, "if you don't have fun you can't come."

Top left: Lonnie Funk, Larry Bouker, Laurie and Dennis Pruett, Darlene and Charlene, Polly Bouker, Sandye and Kent.

We shared many events with our neighbors, Russ and Leslie. We were going out to dinner one night. Leslie and Sandye were in the van waiting for Russ and I to come out of the house. The time delay caused Leslie to leave the van to pull Russ out. Sandye was trying to talk to Leslie, but her words were not comprehensible.

Leslie: "Russ, she is not making any sense. What do I say or do?"

Russ: "You have to just go along and try to help her through it."

Russ would come over to our home to help Sandye with our computer.

Sandye could not type with her hands but wanted to communicate using email. We purchased a software program called, "Dragon Naturally Speaking," which would allow Sandye to speak into the computer. Her words would then be automatically generated. Sandye needed to read a couple paragraphs for the computer to recognize her voice. Russ pulled me aside after trying for two hours.

> Russ: "This is not going to work. Sandye needs to read full sentences at a time and she is not able to do that. She would read the first few words of one sentence and then break to the last words of another sentence."

Frustrated, we abandoned this project. Russ, Leslie, and I realized the limitations and progressions of the disease. Using the computer was a freedom that Sandye had to give up. She was struggling to maintain managing the home. She started to pray specifically for the Lord to restore her brain and thinking to a normal state.

Work was going well as far as my company was aware. I would travel throughout the southeast to conventions, usually held on the beach. Besides showing products at a food show, we would entertain customers at late night activities. One night at Myrtle Beach about twenty people went to a piano dueling bar. One customer was known to drink a lot and I made it my mission to supply his needs. Although he was shocked I kept bringing drinks faster than he could put them away, we drank hard together. Everyone thought it was a game and laughed. The party went past midnight and the group wanted to continue somewhere else. I knew that I had too much to drink. I stumbled across a park near the hotel and fell to the ground. I looked up and saw the sky spinning around. The next thing I remember was waking up the next morning in the park. Drinking had a hold on me.

Somehow that episode was a source of laughter for the work group the next day. To them I was the life of the party. Compulsive behavior needed to be changed to something good. It bothered and embarrassed me to lose control like that.

Brenda was in town for Sandye's birthday. One day they called me downstairs from my office asking about where some of Sandye's jewelry was located. I realized that many of the pieces were missing and could not find them anywhere. After Brenda left, Renae was helping Sandye with the TV on. A news story appeared, which focused on a specific caregiver with her picture on the screen. She had stolen a veteran's war medals. They wanted to know if anyone knew this lady or had items taken.

Renae: "Miss Sandye! Isn't that the caregiver before me?"

Sandye: "Yes, it is. Please turn that volume up and hurry to go get Kent."

We were in shock. The number to call was on the screen. I called and went down to the police station alone. I wanted to protect Sandye. I assumed that our conversation with the detective was recorded as we met in a room. He had two books of photos of jewelry and asked if I recognized anything. At first, I couldn't tell by some of the pictures. Then the picture of the diamond heart that I gave Sandye in Venice was on the page and it was obvious that it had been stolen while Sandye was sleeping. Picture after picture of our jewelry made it very evident that this caregiver had stolen from us. The detective wanted to come to our house to speak to Sandye. He brought a recorder and met her at our kitchen table. While showing the pictures, he came to a charm bracelet.

Policeman: "Do you recognize this?"

Sandye: (gasping) "Yes."

Policeman: "Why is this yours?"

Sandye: "It's my life."

I had bought charms over twenty years from our trips and relationships. Tears began to roll down Sandye's face as she remembered each occasion. One charm was of our cat Cleo and another of the Eiffel Tower. It was heartbreaking. Sandye would give anything away but to steal out of our home was personal. We felt vulnerable and betrayed wondering how to handle future situations, since caregiving was essential. They charged the lady with a felony. She avoided jail, but we did get to see her in court. The judgement was for twenty-three thousand dollars to pay for the items stolen, which has not been paid. Sandye never wanted jewelry after that due to the pain. Nevertheless, I did have a few replacements made, especially the diamond heart. The true memories were kept in our hearts where no one could ever steal them or our joy and memories.

Traditionally, we had big parties at our home on New Years Eve and the Fourth of July. A new neighbor had a band that played in the cul-de-sac during block parties. Our neighbors Ken and Sherri joined in and helped with the fireworks. Reggie and Peggy opened their homes to cook all the food and played the music. They had an amazing home and both couples had big hearts. We invited neighbors, friends and members of our small group to a block party. Though Sandye's health had declined, she wanted us to keep our traditions. The band was playing "Born in the

USA" by Bruce Springsteen, while fireworks exploded overhead. About three hundred people were there. I was drinking beer with my friends, when I started to rethink what I was doing in front of my small group and God. I was being led to be more responsible. This was the first time I united my Christian friends with my old world. After the event, a few neighbors complained to the subdivision about the party getting out of hand. Everyone attending had a great time.

Future parties needed to be scaled down. One thing that I realized was that my Christian friends did not judge me for my drinking habit. I needed to eliminate my extreme behavior because God had made an impression on me. I still hoped to maintain traditions with all of my friends, old and new.

Both Brenda and Margie came at different times to visit. They never met each other. Sandye wanted to spend separate time with each one. Each of them saw Sandye's decline.

Brenda: "When did Sandye stop feeding herself?"

Kent: "Over the last year, she lost strength in her right arm, and it diminished her ability to drive her wheelchair. I started driving her chair for her, finishing her sentences, and feeding her."

I knew she was failing but day-to-day I was not seeing it like Brenda who was coming twice a year. Sandye's father left an inheritance on his passing. Sandye wished to give five thousand dollars to each friend. Brenda and Margie both wanted to reject the gift, but Sandye insisted. It was like she was giving things away before she would leave this earth. They both privately wept trying to cherish every moment with Sandye in joy. It was also a hard pill for me to swallow. As both friends were leaving, they took with them the feeling that they might not see Sandye again.

An older gentleman showed up in our group. His name was Steve Penington. He was our pastor Dustin's father. His wife of fifty years passed away two months before. He did not want to join our group but Dustin insisted, due to his father's deep depression. While we were all on the back porch, Steve stayed back with Sandye. Although Sandye could not complete her sentences, Steve was drawn to her and looked into her eyes. I had a very strong connection with Steve. We had the same sense of humor and I wanted to help him immediately.

I invited him to a men's Bible study that I had attended for the past year held at the community golf course that we lived on. I referred to it as an old man's study. I was the youngest there. These gentlemen were of different religious affiliations. Wayne was Pentecostal and Charles was a Methodist minister. Their leadership made for exciting conversations. We got Steve into playing golf and he became a ranger there. Both groups and our interaction spared his life. To me he became a father figure. The group grew to over twenty men and over half of them were invited to join by Steve.

Even though her disease was causing her to decline, Neta, Tracy and a new marketing friend named Jeff, along with Renae were great support. On some work trips Jeff and I would spend long walks ministering to each other over our personal difficulties. I learned that no matter how difficult things were, being positive and kind paid great dividends. Sandye always taught me not to rehash issues but always to look forward.

Our small group was thriving. Larry and Polly led the way. The group wished to do more. Mike and Brenda went back into prison ministry after several years off. Dennis and Laurie started a nonprofit program for handicapped people. Dennis had a college friend named Chris Jarod, who had Muscular Dystrophy and needed a lot of help. Chris was about two and one-half hours away. Dennis formed a group to travel to rebuild Chris' home. The group numbered from ten to as many as twenty people, all willing to drive for five hours and put in a hard day's work. They built a shower and an additional bedroom. Air conditioning and electrical upgrades were made along with a track system that provided an overhead lift to transfer Chris from the bedroom to the shower. Lonny, Kathy and a few single ladies were invited to our group. Sharon had MS. Janice struggled with a cane. An elder in the church, named Rene, and his wife Evelyn played a integral part in keeping the group involved in church activities. The spirit of this group was widely known and infectious in the church. Oh! Don't forget Steve. He was now the life of the party and absolutely loved Sandye.

Due to Sandye's decline, I didn't feel comfortable leaving her overnight without someone there. I let the small group know that we were looking for someone to stay in the upstairs bedroom, previously vacated by Lacey and J.B. Larry had a manager who would be a good fit for our home. At the right time, he wanted us to meet her. Her name was Brandy Thomas.

For the past two years communication with Sandye became more and more difficult. It was second nature for me to complete her sentences. Her body could not maintain a vertical position and she needed pillows to prop her up for support. Renae, our caregiver dressed her every day. Although Sandye was declining, she kept her strong will to get things done. Her most important desire was to get baptized by emersion in a lake. I knew she wanted to communicate that, but her words came out in pieces.

Sandye: "The lake."

Kent: "Do you want to get baptized?"

Sandye: "Baptized."

Kent: "Do you want me to get someone from the church to get you baptized?"

Sandye: "The Lake."

Kent: "Outside in a lake?"

Sandye: "Soon."

This was a difficult time but I was happy to communicate with her. Steve was over for a meeting one Sunday afternoon. Sandye looked at him intently.

Sandye: "Baptized."

Steve: "What does she want?"

Kent: "Sandye wants to get baptized in full submersion in a lake."

Steve: "That's something that I can make happen. I know someone who can get this done." (with a wide smile)

The church was started in Steve's house before he donated the land across the street to build a new church for his son, Dustin. Behind Steve's house was a lake where Dustin baptized his father three years before. Over the next three years, Dustin had baptized over three-hundred people in that lake.

> Steve: (looking at Sandye with a smile) "We'll get this done, Sandye. We will get you baptized."

Sandye nodded intently with a sense of urgency.

In May of two-thousand-sixteen, Sandye was approaching her fifty-ninth birthday. Brenda was coming as usual. I took Sandye for her monthly infusion prior to her arrival. During the infusion, Sandye told me that she wanted to do something really fun with Brenda in two days. She then said she wanted to go ziplining. It was going to be tough to find anyone or place in the state that would accept the challenge. I located a place in Helen, Georgia, that had one zip line that went a half mile. They said that they would do what it took to give her the experience. On arrival, we had to go through a lot of preparation to get her into a harness. That was difficult from a sitting position. I lifted her into an open-air jeep and we rode along with Brenda up the mountain. At the top of the mountain, I took the wheelchair from the jeep. Then I lifted Sandye out of the jeep onto the chair. With three people lifting the chair holding Sandye we were able to climb sixteen steps to the zipline platform. Backing up every step seemed dangerous. It was obvious that this was the first time they attempted this feat. We were relieved and exhausted when we reached the top of the steps and the platform.

From the platform there were two parallel zip lines. One man went down first to position himself at the bottom to catch us. Brenda went down at the same time on the other line. Another went on the second line with her. Sandye's senses also diminished, so I wasn't sure if she would get the whole experience. As she was ready to go, she tried to talk to me but the words didn't come out. I reassured her that it would be fine. We counted down, three, two, one and off she went. The sound of the wire and pulleys was loud. A thrilling feeling came over me as I screamed.

Kent: "Yehaw! She did it. She, actually did it. She could have died ten times over but not today!!!"

It was exhilarating! Now here she is ziplining. Then we went after her. It was a thrilling ride over the trees. You could hear the metal screeching as we flew down the mountain. Leaves of trees brushed my feet. Coming to a screeching halt on a ten-story platform, I could see Sandye being held tightly until I arrived. Ten flights of stairs led to the ground. The only way for her to get to the ground was by repelling her down using a cord. This experience was like one unexpected ride or challenge after another. Looking down, I could see them drop her directly into the wheelchair. That was nearly a disaster as the wheelchair almost broke her leg. I screamed and ran down the ten stories to assist. The fact that they would take the risk to allow her the opportunity was special. We took a picture of everyone with Sandye wearing the birthday hat. It was a memorable birthday.

When we got home, Sandye was exhausted. She went straight to bed. The next day I asked about her experience.

Sandye: "Zip line?"

Kent: "Yes, that was fun, wasn't it?"

Sandye: (with a confused look) "Go zipline."

Kent: "Do you mean that you want to go zipline?"

Sandye: "Yes!"

Then I realized that she did not remember it, which broke my heart. Later, when we showed her pictures, she would smile.

On June 12, 2016, Steve fulfilled Sandye's wish. The date for her baptism had finally come. That Sunday we went to church and felt a time of excitement. Sandye was going to get her wish. She had been baptized before with me with a sprinkle on the forehead at the Methodist Church, but she was adamant about being fully submersed. After church, we met behind Steve's house at the lake. There were about thirty people present including our whole home group and close friends. A white robe was placed on Sandye. I knew she was happy, despite her body language slumping hard to the right. Larry and Polly came up with another well-dressed lady.

Larry: "I would like you to meet Brandy. She is the lady that I told you about that might be able to live upstairs."

Kent: "It's very nice to meet you,"

Brandy: "Miss Sandye. It's very nice to meet you. I look forward to your baptism. I feel honored to be invited to this event. We can talk later at your home."

Dustin: (feeling the intensity in the air) "I would like to stop and pray with you."

Everyone gathered around Sandye. Those standing close placed their hands on her head. The rest touched shoulders. Everyone was connected. Dustin prayed like it came from the Holy Spirit. We then pushed the wheelchair down the rocky slope to the edge of the lake.

Sandye: "Stop!"

Kent: "What is it, honey? What do you need?"

Sandye: "No wheelchair."

Kent: "Sandye doesn't want the wheelchair to define her. We must pick her up and carry her into the lake."

Five men from our small group lifted her up and carried her into the water where Dustin was waiting. The others watched from the bank with incredible excitement. This is something that Sandye wanted for a long time. The moment brought closure and a strong sense of fulfillment. There was an amazing brotherhood bond as Dustin submerged her under the water. As we carried her back to her chair, Sandye mustered up one big smile and cheers erupted from everyone. I drove the van down to the wheelchair, loaded it and went directly home to get changed. Everyone came to our house for food, fellowship, and a great celebration. Something very special just happened. Sandye could not smile much anymore but you could sense a great feeling of relief for her.

Baptizing Sandye (Lonnie, Rene, Kent, Pastor Dustin, Larry, and Dennis)

Brandy came to live upstairs with us soon after and helped with caregiving while I was out of town. A man named Paul moved into the basement with his daughter Tori and seemed to be a good fit. We would share personal struggles and help each other where needed.

Our small group was thriving. We started inviting other neighbors with prayer needs to join us. Ken, a principal across the street who helped with the fireworks at the block parties, was diagnosed with cancer. He had adopted three children. His wife Sherry was very concerned about their children along with Ken. He came over and shared about his cancer. I asked if we could pray for him. Other neighbors named, Pete and Cocoa, also came over asking for prayer for family needs. Others in the group started bringing people over for personal prayer over the summer. God was positively affecting the neighborhood. These times created a strong feeling in the group to do more.

In August of two-thousand-sixteen, our small group met after church. Sandye attended, although incoherent. Chris Jarod came to our home with his wife and daughter. They drove three hours to thank our group for all the work that was done in his home. Because our home was handicap accessible, the Jarods were able to enter. Chris' wife Debbie and daughter, Krystal, sang in his church and brought some songs to sing to us. Humbly, he shared that they were struggling with financial needs. Our van fund had accrued seven thousand dollars. There was great emotion and spirit in the room that was powerfully moving. While Brandy was helping Sandye, I went over to them.

Kent: "Sandye, we have enough money to get a handicapped van for somebody. This would be our fifth give away. I would like to give this family the money as our next project."

Sandye nodded with approval.

Kent: "Let me have everyone's attention. We would like to use the money for our next van give away and give it to the Jarod family."

Larry: "Why don't you make that an even ten thousand. We will add three thousand to the fund."

Debby, Chris' wife, ran across the room, fell to her knees into Chris' lap as he sat in his wheelchair. She broke down in uncontrollable tears. The pressure of being a caregiver and their financial needs were overwhelming. At the brink of desperation, they were saved again, but we knew that it was of the Lord. You could feel the excitement flood the room. The rest of the afternoon was a joyous explosion. Everyone left filled with hope, love for one another and with God. As I put Sandye to bed, I prayed with her about the overwhelming presence of the Holy Spirit in our house. She felt that joy as well.

Two weeks later she shared with me.

Sandye: "I'm tired."

Kent: "Let me turn the light off so you can get some rest."

Sandye: (with a stern voice) "NO! I'm tired." (drawn out low tone)

I knew by her tone that she didn't have much more to give. She was not giving up, but her body had reached its limit.

The MS center wanted to feature Sandye in their September magazine. They thought she was the model for a positive attitude while overcoming the most difficult conditions. The center sent me a questionnaire to fill out. I would read the question to her. She looked at me knowing that I knew the answer that she could not utter. The questions about MS I answered for her with "MS does not define me." She would look at me and nod with approval as if to say, "That's right." She believed that God did not give her MS but he was the first one there when she got it. They ran the article with a picture from the past. In that same magazine, a new physician's assistant, Kathleen Clark (Katie), was featured and became our new PA with Dr. Stuart. She was very kind and could relate to Sandye, despite the communication issues.

Over the previous year, we had not attended church more than a couple of times. Our small group came after church to our home. We were able to watch the service over the internet. One Sunday in September we were able to attend church. The pastor asked if people needed prayer and if so, to come forward. Surprisingly, Sandye nudged me with her right hand. I leaned over and she whispered.

Sandye: "Take me."

This was totally out of character. As we moved towards the front, our entire group followed with others to pray over her. It was at the end of the service and continued for a long time. Sandye kept her head down and soaked it all in. I stepped aside in awe of what was happening. Rene, the church elder and member of group, approached me.

Rene: "Kent, we have not done a good job as a congregation in praying for Sandye. That stops right now. We will pray together to get her health and healing as a group with the Lord. We take back the responsibility to pray, firmly believing that God can do anything and is going to help Sandye."

His intense look into my eyes, inspired hope in me that I never had before. We left the church that day feeling something special from God.

***

Chip, chip, chip... Faith takes a leap as people share, pray, and help one another. Sandye needs me more than ever. Church, friends and neighbor fellowship takes on new direction and meaning. The marble slab now has a solid foundation, and Kent has found that rock of support from God. Alcohol still is an imperfection and a work in progress.

Miracles

On Sunday 9/25/2016, our group was over for the normal meeting. Sandye had been going downhill physically and mentally for a long time now. At this time, she was also experiencing a lot of pain in her body and head. We tried every medicine available with no relief. Then it was my time to speak.

> Kent: "I must be honest with you. I understand why some people in this world use a doctor like, Dr. Kevorkian on the west coast." (He was a doctor, that was known for giving patients drugs that would help them die peacefully.)

Sandye had indicated to me over the summer that she was running out of energy and was very tired. I just did not want to see her suffer and she had no quality of life at this time. Sandye sat the entire meeting not saying a word and looking miserable, for she was experiencing internal pain. As we were finishing up, one of the ladies, seeing the obvious situation, asked Sandye if it was ok for everyone to pray for her? To that Sandye nodded with approval. All the ladies moved around Sandye, laid their hands on her and began to pray intensely for healing. You could feel their sense of urgency as they prayed. After a good bit of time, I stepped back into the kitchen. Rene, the elder from the Church who previously prayed for

Sandye at the church service, began speaking.

Rene: "Kent, how long has she been in this much pain?"

Kent: "A few weeks. She does not like to burden people."

Rene: (Looking me in the eyes very seriously) "Kent, we cannot help you if you don't let us know what is happening. Prayer is crucial to the healing process. You must tell us in order for this church family to help you."

Kent: "Okay, I will."

Rene: "I mean it Kent!" (Grabbing me by the arm)

I could feel the importance of this moment as I assured him that I would open up to them when needed. I took Sandye back to bed immediately after they left, praying to the Lord for resolution.

The next day Sandye seemed a little better and was more receptive. So, I decided to go ahead and leave for Tennessee on a day trip. On Tuesday 9/27/2016, I left home at five AM to get up to Tennessee and back all in one day. I made it to Knoxville, Tennessee, for an appointment with six ladies at ten AM at the Knox County School. I was on my way back to our home which was a four-hour drive when Renae, our caregiver, called me.

Renae: "Mr. Kent (she called me Mr. Kent out of respect, which to this day feels kind of odd), please hurry home. Mrs. Sandye is really very sick."

Kent: "I will be home in less than two hours. Will she be alright until I get there"

Renae: "Mr. Kent this is serious, she has some type of infection and does not look good"

Kent: "Do you need to call 911?"

Renae: "She won't let me call anyone. Please just come home fast."

I felt the urgency in her voice and drove straight to the house when it started to rain. As I quickly ran into the bedroom, I looked Sandye in the eyes and could see she was not herself. She was not talking and distant. I had seen this look before and knew it was urgent to get her to the hospital. I physically maneuvered her over to the wheelchair and hurried out to the car. I transferred her into the front seat (with her being unstable it was better to have her next to me inside the car rather than strapping the wheelchair down in the van) and put the manual wheelchair in the trunk of the car. Then I went back into the house and quickly packed everything necessary to stay overnight at the hospital (I knew this drill from before and prepared for any result). Renae, who had become very close to Sandye, watched intently as we left for the hospital. It was forty-five minutes to get to Piedmont Hospital (which was connected to the Shepard Center where the MS Center was originally started). There were many Hospitals closer but we felt comfortable being close to all our specialists.

The rain was getting heavier and heavier on the drive. I tried to comfort Sandye but she was not responding, which alerted me that she needed critical care. After the tough week that she had before, I knew she needed immediate care as soon as we arrived at the hospital. I pulled up to the emergency room in a downpour and moved under the overhang. I signaled the employee at the front desk to come out and help me. The ER waiting area was crammed full and I knew Sandye could not wait in that line to see the doctor. The employee came running out with one of the hospitals wheelchairs, I shouted, as the rain was beating a loud drum sounding noise on the carport.

Kent: "Please! Go and get a hospital gurney bed. She is in very bad shape and needs special help in the back room."

Employee: (Seeing Sandye slumped over in the seat) "She needs to get in this wheelchair and go in the main area to get checked in."

Kent: (as the rain was pelleting the roof, I was screaming to be heard) "She cannot walk, I have to lift her out of the car, she has a serious infection and is in trouble, PLEASE! Go get a gurney. She needs to be seen right now!"

The employee held firm, and probably thought that we were just another customer trying to move pass all the other sick patients.

Employee: (Screaming to be heard over the downpour) "Get her into the wheelchair."

Kent: "Get a hospital Bed" (I have never had this type of

urgency before)

Employee: "Get her into the chair"

Kent: (At the top of my lungs) "SHE NEEDS TO SEE A DOCTOR NOW!"

Right that instant, I large lightning bolt caromed down over the hospital with an immediate huge deafening crash of thunder right behind it. The employee ducked down and froze. As he rose back up to his feet with a look of terror in his eyes, he immediately said I will go get a hospital bed. I thought to myself as I looked at motionless Sandye, "Wow! Did that just happen?" I didn't care as long as they expedited this process. That's all that we needed. A bed was brought out with another attendant. I still had to lift her out of the car, knowing they could mishandle her. She was dead weight and a struggle to lift her onto the bed. They took her back into the ER area where ambulances bring people. There were no rooms available and sick people lined up and down the hallway. After checking her in, a doctor came and looked Sandye over. She was conscious but not responding.

Doctor: "I see she has a serious issue."

He said that he was sorry, but we would have to wait for a room to come available in the ER. They would see how quickly they could fit her in. They could not treat her in the cramped hallway, so we waited, and waited, and waited. After three hours, at about midnight, they finally moved us into an ER room. They then hooked up an IV and gave her fluids, antibiotics and started doing all kinds of tests. Every step took a long time because they were so busy. The doctor had said they were going to try to admit her into the hospital when a room became available. I prayed hard for direction and mercy. The night now stretched into the morning. It was now 7:30 AM. A new doctor came in:

Doctor: "Hi Sandra, can you hear me?"

She gave no response. You could tell that Sandye was too fatigued to speak. She was consciously looking at the doctor but could not express herself. I had become accustomed to speaking for her over the last couple of years.

Kent: "She has been like this all night."

Doctor: "My name is Dr. Bielo and I will be Sandra's doctor up on the floor once she gets a room. For now, the ER doctor wants to move her to the ICU, because her blood pressure is dropping. I could see that now it is 80 over 50, which is very low. They said it would be a while to get in there and it would be okay for me to take a break."

I stepped outside where we had originally come into the ER the night before. It was now a clear crisp morning. I remembered the voice of Rene a couple of days before urging me to call him, I dialed his number at the beginning of the workday, knowing he had a busy job not expecting him to answer. He picked up the phone.

Rene: "I know if you called me, it is serious Kent."

Kent: "Hi Rene. I am at Piedmont Hospital. Sandye is in

trouble. She has some type of infection. Her Blood pressure has dropped to a dangerous level. They are ready to move her to ICU and I don't know what to pray for. I am ready to give up and let her go. It is getting too hard for her and gut wrenching for me to endure."

Renae: "Kent, listen to me. We have dominion over our pets and can make decisions for them, but God has dominion over us! That means that we have to pray hard for God's healing right now. Listen to me, I am going to pray."

As I walked all over the parking lot, Rene began praying. Then we both prayed compassionately for God's direction and healing mercy. I held my hand in the air with my eyes closed holding on to every word that we prayed together, until I heard the word "amen."

Rene: "Kent. Go back in there with conviction to God's plan. I am going to call the whole small group and Pastor Dustin to set prayer into action. Just remember, there will be people praying all over the place right now for Sandye."

I felt much better. I had a resolve and strength that I really needed at the time. I returned to the ER with a new confidence for a positive outcome. I walked back into the ER room and looked at the blood pressure machine. Sandye's blood pressure had now dropped to the life-threatening level. It was now sixty-nine over thirty-nine (I since learned that she could have passed away at any moment). The nurse popped her head into the room and said they were clearing a room and would be coming soon to take her to the ICU. I started texting Rene and Steve to specifically get everyone to pray for her blood pressure to go up. I put my hand on Sandye's arm and started praying out loud with passion to God for his help. Knowing that many people were praying simultaneously, I focused my prayer specifically on her blood pressure. Over the next forty-five minutes, to my astonishment, her blood pressure slowly started to rise. The doctors had not added any new medicine and there had been nothing but decline over the night. As her blood pressure was rising, I was texting to Steve and Rene that it was working and to send messages to keep praying. After forty-five minutes, her blood pressure was now all the way back up to ninety over sixty. It was amazing to watch this happen right before my eyes. There was a supernatural feeling in the room. The ER Doctor came into the room.

Doctor: "Okay, we are going to take her now to the ICU."

Seeing a significant change in her blood pressure stopped the doctor in his tracks.

Doctor: "Wait a minute. What is happening here?"

He looked at all his charts to see if there were any orders or medication that he did not know about. He looked up with a puzzled look of astonishment. He left the room, totally confused and came back a moment later.

Doctor: "Due to her sudden improvement, we are going to now move her up to a room in hospital." (Shaking his head in disbelief)

I just smiled knowing something special had happened and did not care because Sandye was now out of the woods. At noon on Wednesday 9/28, we were moved up to the hospital floor. I now was watching Sandye rapidly come back to her normal self. We started laughing and talking about another trip we might take one day. Dr. Bielo, the doctor we had met that morning, was now attending to us. She came into the room that afternoon.

Dr. Beilo: "Sandra!" (She said with an alert voice)

Sandye: "Yes, Ma'am." (now speaking clearly like she was normal)

Dr. Bielo: (shocked again at Sandye being able to speak) "Sandra. I cannot believe the color you now have in your face and life in your body. Now you are speaking to me as if you were out for a walk. I have never seen such a swift turn-around."

She looked at me and I shrugged my shoulders not knowing what to say. Sandye just smiled.

Sandye: "God is good all the time."

The doctor looked her over and just shook her head in disbelief. They wanted to keep her another night administering antibiotics and to observe her. I constantly kept our whole prayer group in the loop with everything that was happening. There were many thankful celebrations to God that night.

The next two days were equally hopeful as the doctors were shocked with Sandye's improvement. On Friday, the doctor came in to speak to us.

> Dr. Bielo: "Sandy. We were going to let you go home before the weekend, but a couple of the tests show that you might have a blood disease. That totally contradicts the fact that you are acting and feeling so well now."

Nothing was surprising me at this point.

> Dr. Bielo: "We are going to keep you over the weekend until we get back the blood test results."

Sandye and I decided to make the best of this time and discuss our next big trip together around the world. As we shared we laughed and reminisced. Saturday, October first, Sandye was not her normal self. She looked at me with a concerning face.

> Kent: "What's wrong?"

> Sandye: "I don't know. I just feel weird."

I thought that maybe she might have missed one of her normal medicines which could have caused this reaction. I realized that she had not taken estrogen all week thinking this might be the cause. I knew that I had brought all of her normal medicines which were in the car.

Kent: "Hold on. I will go out to the car."

Sandye: (worried) "Hurry."

I ran to the car, sensing something urgent, got her medicines and hurried back to the room. It was now 10:30. When I approached her, she looked asleep. I called out her name several times and she was noncoherent. I called the nurse in, whose name was Carly. Her parents were both Methodist ministers. She had only been a nurse for three months. When she looked into Sandye's eyes, she was startled. Sandye's eyes had rolled back into her head. She immediately called a special code for help. A team of people came in and noticed the "Do not resuscitate" bracelet on Sandye's wrist. Doctor Bielo came in soon after.

Nurse: "Did you see her eyes?"

Dr. Bielo: "Yes."

Both had a look of confusion as to what to do next. Sandye was still breathing but did not seem to be conscious.

Dr. Bielo: "Let's order a brain scan. Take her down stat and get some results."

As all this was happening, I sat down and prayed. Because of what happened earlier, I knew to reach out to our prayer group. I called Steve.

Kent: "Steve. (with my voice cracking with nervousness) It's an emergency. Sandye is noncoherent and needs immediate prayer."

Steve: "I'm on it. I will call Pastor Dustin and the rest of the group to pray now."

I was focused on my resolve to get as many prayer warriors involved, although others said that I was very calm. Sandye went down for her brain scan at 11:00. With the room empty, I called Rene from church. He was in Tennessee with his wife Evelyn at a baby shower. He knew something had to be wrong and took my call.

Kent: "Rene. I don't know what's wrong with Sandye but she seems to be in a coma. All I know is that we need to unite in prayer."

Rene prayed like fire for several minutes as I paced up and down the hallway. Afterwards, he said that he would reach out to as many as possible for prayer. My phone lit up with text messages. At least seven different states showed people praying. Sandye returned to the room at 11:30, still appearing as though she was in a coma. Everyone left the room as there was nothing for them to do. She was breathing fine but nonresponsive. I saw Dr. Bielo outside the room as if something was going to happen. I started singing to Sandye some of her favorite songs.

Kent: "Jesus, Jesus, precious Jesus..." and "It is well, with my soul"

I kissed her on the lips.

Kent: "Sandye. We still have many things left to do. Trips, van gifts, ..."

Now at 11:55 her eyes started to squint and tears started to flow. Her face began to tighten. I called the doctor and Nurse Carly to come back in the room. Tears flowed freely from her eyes. Her face remained distorted.

Kent: "What's happening?"

Dr. Bielo: "She's trying to wake up. Can you hear me?"

Sandye's eyes slowly opened. She nodded her head with approval.

Dr. Bielo: "Move your fingers."

Sandye moved her second finger up and down.

Dr. Bielo: "What's your name?"

Sandye: "Sandye."

We waited a few moments as her face tightened even more. She began to cry profusely. We were all taken back as to why she was weeping.

Kent: "Sandye. Why are you crying?"

Sandye: (after a moment) "Jesus sent me back for Him and I didn't want to come."

We were shocked. The rest of us stared at each other with a stunned look.

Sandye: "I saw my mom in her green apron."

When I told her sister Mary that she had seen their mother in her green apron she just cried when she finally spoke to Sandye days later.

Mary: "You saw Mommy in her green apron? You know that was when she was in the happiest time of her life cooking for the whole family."

Mary held this close to heart when she heard this. Again, Sandye started crying. Dr. Bielo told us to let her have some time to gather herself. I was so glad that she was awake. I let her rest and did not get much sleep myself. I contemplated all that just happened. Early the next morning I was asking God to tell me what just happened. What did I witness? A clear message came to me.

"You have witnessed a miracle by the power of prayer to God."

It gave me great comfort although I had a sense of unbelief. I called Wayne, the leader of the men's Bible study at the golf course.

Wayne: "This must be important. I don't usually answer the

phone at 7am on Sunday."

I walked him through all that had happened. Wayne was a Pentecostal minister. Over his eighty years he had seen and heard many things, but this was amazing. He reassured me that God was doing something truly wonderful here. Later that morning, Sandye was calm, tired and distant. It was obvious to me that she had been through something very rare. The doctor came in.

Kent: "Doctor. What exactly happened yesterday?"

Dr. Bielo: "When we came in the room, we saw both of Sandra's pupils were blown, which meant that her brain was not responding. So, we sent her down for a brain scan with the thought that a tumor existed, blocking the message from her brain to her body. Her body seemed to be working fine. The results showed that no tumor was present. Sandye, your brain was not functioning, but your body was fine. That is not medically possible." She paused for a few seconds and then said "You are a medical miracle."

We were blown away by those words. Sandye held these precious moments close to her heart and knew more than we could ever imagine. It was all too much and would take months and even years for her to talk about her experience. The whole next day, I had to keep the room dark and everyone out. She was extremely sensitive to the light. I spoke to the staff in the hallway. We were in unchartered territory and they had no answers. They appeared uncomfortable.

Dr. Bielo: "I think we need to discharge her as there is nothing else for us to do. Oh, by the way, the blood disease is completely gone."

That Tuesday, she was discharged. While preparing her to leave the room, Sandye was still overwhelmed and sensitive. I made a pit stop to the rest room and returned. Sandye appeared to be asleep. I thought she might have left us again. I touched her hands, and her eyes opened. That gave me a huge sigh of relief.

Kent: "Where were you?"

Sandye: "My dad was messing with me. He's such a card." (a smile came to her face)

Kent: (Not believing what I was hearing) "Yes. He was a funny man and loved you dearly."

Her dad passed away eight years earlier, but she felt him near at that moment and off an on throughout the rest of the day. We had to get an overdue infusion at the MS clinic on the way home. During that time, her dad was helping her through it, although unaware to me at the time. She shared the moments later. Renae was the perfect person to meet us at home. Sandye needed calmness. Renae had a great sense for what Sandye needed would sit with Sandye for eight hours without words being spoken. I cannot sit for five minutes without talking. It was exactly what Sandye needed.

While Sandye rested at home I knew that she was okay. I did not want to miss a work event at the Gwinnett County School District, which is the largest in the state of Georgia. The school foodservice director Karen Hallford and chef Rachel met me. I shared with them that I had seen a miracle without giving many details. They felt my emotion and were very compassionate. Karen was very supportive of us for years and we deeply appreciated her kindness.

My men's group and our small group were buzzing about what God was doing, remaining in deep prayer. Pastor Dustin asked to come by the following Saturday to see her. Up until that time, I did not allow visitation.

Dustin: "What was it like being with Jesus?"

Sandye: "I had my head on His lap. We were loving on each other."

As she was sharing, you could feel the Holy Spirit in the room.

Sandye: "Love, love, so much love and joy."

Dustin: "You didn't want to come back?"

Sandye: (crying) "No."

Dustin: "Sandye. I could preach the rest of my life from a podium and you could bring more people to Christ from this bed. Would it be okay if I shared your story with Kent in the service tomorrow?"

Sandye: "Yes." (agreed)

That night, I spent some time with our upstairs guest, Brandy. We played some deep Christian songs about miracles. Brandy agreed to stay home with Sandye and watch the service livestream in bed with her. Before the service, I was in the backroom praying with the elders that God would cover all that was said that day. I wasn't sure what to say or not say. After speaking for twenty-three minutes, the congregation was extremely quiet. You could feel an intense power of the Lord over the room. People flooded to the front for prayer at the end.

Lady: "When you talked about the lightning bolt, I knew God was speaking to me."

I had no idea that I mentioned that, but I knew that God placed those words on my mouth. When I returned home, Sandye was content with the delivery of her story. Brandy, a part time pastor, knew that she was witnessing something very special and was a great encourager.

Sandye was speaking more fluently but I was not fully aware of it with all the week's events. The following week was filled with more recovery. Wayne, from the men's group, asked me to tell the testimony. The word was out and the men's group tripled. I felt an incredible presence of the Lord during this time. They asked if there was a song that could be played before the group started. My favorite song by Mercy Me, was "I Can Only Imagine." As I relived the last two weeks, the men cried, gasped and were unbelievably moved over the next hour. Thoughts came to me like:

...Why would God pick me?

...Doesn't He know who I was before I met Sandye?

...I don't deserve this.

Wayne: "He knows your heart. Look at all the Biblical examples of imperfect men: Moses, who stuttered, Saul killed Christians, and David, who took Bathsheba and had her husband killed."

Kent: "I guess I should be saying, 'Why not me,' huh?"

After sharing Sandye's story with the church, they put it out on livestream. All my family watched. It weighed heavy, since most were unbelievers. Russ and Leslie watched with their family and were also quiet. Neta, from my workplace, who covered for me many times over the last six months and was now a very good friend, decided to watch the livestream from California. I spoke with her the next day.

Neta: "Kent. I thought my TV was going to catch fire because church was on in my house but thank you for sharing."

She was agnostic until this time.

Kent: (laughed) "You'll be alright."

I knew that a seed had been planted and God would do the rest.

A man named, Taylor, from the men's group approached me after the meeting and asked if I would come to his men's group and speak the next day. I went to the back of a restaurant in a private room and met twenty more guys the next morning at seven AM. As I cried and relived the moment again, the men powerfully praised God. I found it interesting that they called their group, "Knuckleheads for Christ." I began to support both groups afterwards.

The next day, Sandye started sharing about a girl that we had been praying for from Louisiana with cancer, named Melissa.

Sandye: "Melissa's spirit was in a good place."

Kent: "When did you see her?"

Sandye: "I didn't see her but felt her presence when I was coming back after my visit with Jesus. It was like I was returning and she was going to be with Him."

That Sunday, as I was leaving for church, my phone beeped a message that Melissa had passed away. I ran back in to tell Sandye. She had a big smile as it to say, "I already knew." During the week she was getting stronger and more alert. Previously, after any hospital visit, it took months for her to get out of bed due to the MS. In less than two weeks, she was ready to see our Sunday group, which had tripled since her last visit.

Rene: "Sandye. You look so good."

The previous year, she slumped hard over her wheelchair. The last few months hardly brought out a smile. Now she was sitting up. Her skin shined like a China doll. Her smile was vibrant.

Sandye: (smiling) "Well, what do you think about that?"

To the people in the room, it was an immediate transformation. She looked twenty-five years younger. Over the next three weeks, other positive changes appeared with Sandye. Her close friend Karen came over to our kitchen table. Sandye took a fork and stabbed some sweet potatoes and put it in her mouth. It had been three years since she was able to feed herself. Both she and Karen laughed. I turned a recorder on, which prompted Sandye to act like she was going to flick the next bite of potatoes on me.

Kent: "You haven't been able to feed yourself in three years. You know that, right?"

She looked at her friend and smiled without a word said. On another day we were in the kitchen when I heard her electric wheelchair beep. I was alarmed because she had not driven her chair for several years. The next thing I knew was she was driving over to me. It blew my mind. Later, I came home from work and Renae came out of the house in tears. This took me back as she never cried.

Kent: "What's wrong?"

Renae: "I just can't believe it. Last year, were trying to put together Sandye's Thanksgiving shopping list. Because she

couldn't get her words out, it took two full days to complete
the list. She just completed the list for this year in ten minutes."

She shook her head and walked to the car. Her tears were of amazement,
joy and awe of the Lord.

On another occasion I was working upstairs and headed downstairs for a
drink. I could hear Sandye doing devotions with Renae. She was reading at
full speed like she had done more than five years before. I couldn't believe
my ears. I sat down on the stairs and wept. She prayed for her brain and
God answered her prayer. I took her to a reading clinic where she read from
a book while I videotaped it. I sent it to Russ, who had attempted to get
her to read before. Immediately, he called me.

Russ: "What in the world?"

Prior, Russ was not interested in attending church. I could feel God's
pull as I shared story after story. There was no doubt we were seeing an
undeniable miracle.

We had an appointment with Dr. Stuart, the neurologist, to go over all
that had happened. Katie, the Physicians Assistant, met us first. Sandye
drove the wheelchair in and spun it around, causing Katy's eyes to pop
wide open. Prior to that, I would drive the chair in with Sandye slumped
over and I would do all the speaking. We told her the story and she broke
down in tears. That was a common reaction from most that I told the story
too. Dr. Stuart entered the room and had already been briefed by Katie.

Sandye: "Hello young man."

Sandye had not been able to speak to him in sentences over the past two years. He was amazed. I told him a shortened version of the story.

Dr. Stuart: (searching for answers) "What medication has been changed over the last six months?"

Kent: "We haven't changed anything in years."

I asked Sandye to hold the water bottle. She grabbed it and drank from it.

Dr. Stuart: "How many years has it been since she did that?"

Kent: "Several."

He could see the mental and physical difference, immediately. Sandye answered every question, while cutting me off abruptly. I was used to completing her sentences.

Kent: "What do you make of this?"

Dr. Stuart: "I have been doing this over fifty years. But for to see someone transform so drastically both mentally and physically? I have never seen or heard of this happening. My faith is one thing, but medically, there is no answer."

He left the room in awe. Katy, on the next visit, cried again in disbelief.

Katy: "Sandye. We thought you were fading and were going to die. We thought we had lost you. It's unbelievable."

Kent: "What has the doctor shared with his constituents?"

Katy: "It doesn't matter. It's on your chart. It says, '***marked medical improvement with no medical reason***'."

At the end of the month, on Leslie's sixtieth birthday, Russ asked for videos from those who could not come to their Nantucket vacation resort. We complied with a video of Sandye and I singing a rapid-fire video. Sandye did not miss a beat.

We sang the traditional birthday song and then usually followed it with the Beatles version of "Today's your birthday, da na na na na. na, na , (sing along if you know it). At the end of the video, Sandye spoke.

Sandye: "It's me."

It had been years since they heard her talk sentences, let alone sing.

Kent: "Did you get our Birthday salutation for Leslie?" Just wanting to check and see if they received it.

Russ: "Kent, we were blown away. It was the best present Leslie could have received. How in the world could she sing like that? We have no words but are thankful."

I knew this was changing their family in a good way.

Later, we went to church. Sandye drove her chair up to a table and asked the lady for information on women's groups. She took the pamphlet and drove off. The lady appeared as though she had seen a ghost. Her jaw was wide open.

Kent: "What's wrong?"

Lady: "I have prayed with Sandye for two years without ever hearing her say a word. She was always motionless."

***

Chip, chip, chip, God speaks to us in an unmistakable spiritual voice, especially when we are open to listen. Witnessing a miracle will certainly get our attention. Medical science has limitations, but none exist with God. God uses ordinary people to do extraordinary things for Him. Fervent prayer is never in vain. The artistic work as it appears to radiate as if to glorify the master creator.

Soaring with Jesus

S andye's miracles and the following testimonies brought new life to many church families. All the men's prayer groups grew and became exponentially more involved in everyday lives. The couple's ministry I was involved with on Sunday also took off.

Before Thanksgiving, Sandye felt sick to her stomach and had a tough time keeping food down. She had a lot of pain in her abdomen. Usually, I would take her to the hospital, but this was too volatile. I called 9-1-1. The ambulance driver wanted to take her to a local hospital. I insisted that they take her downtown to Piedmont. I went with her. While enroute, Sandye was in severe pain. They could not administer any medication until they reached the hospital. Before arriving, she passed out. The ER technician in the ambulance tried to wake her up using standard protocol. She finally awoke.

Sandye: "Oh, it hurts so much. Why did you wake me up?"

ER: "I couldn't leave you unconscious. It's my job."

I felt helpless and tried to give her comfort. Extreme pain is a game changer. At the hospital, dilaudid was administered as a pain medicine, which had a side effect that caused her whole body to react sensitively. They admitted her and after two days of testing, the pain continued. I reached out to the Friday men's group and asked for music or scriptures to help us through. On the third night at two in the morning, Sandye consistently asked me to place an ice bath all over her neck and body to freeze her skin to counteract the pain. It hurt so bad that the ice helped. I played different songs that the men sent. Then I played "It is Well" by Christine DiMarco. Sandye felt a sense of relief when she heard it.

Sandye: (after the song ended) "Play it again, now!"

I played that song for four hours straight and felt that it saved her that night. After five days I still wore the same clothes. I needed to get a shower, change my clothes and bring her handicap needs. I called my friend Steve to get his son, Pastor Dustin, to meet me after the service. It was now Sunday. I looked terrible, smelled bad and was not very presentable entering the church. I sat down and my whole prayer group gathered around me. Pastor Dustin got down on his knees in front of me, placed his hands on my feet and led the prayer for Sandye's healing. This time of prayer along with the others from the two men's groups was keeping me afloat. After getting cleaned up, I returned to the hospital with a new feeling as if I was reenergized.

On the sixth day, the doctors were still at a loss. A baclofen pump had been placed in her stomach to counteract spasms that occurred many times a day in the past. The specialist that installed the pump insisted that the pump was not the cause of her pain. He said it was just a metal cylinder but he would remove it if we insisted and would return the next day for our decision.

Kent: "Sandye, I am not sure what to do here, but I think you need that surgery."

Sandye: "Call our prayer group and ask them to pray. Let them help us make the decision."

I made the calls. After prayer, everyone felt that the surgery was the best option. I felt like I was playing God and did not feel comfortable being forced to make this decision. The next morning the doctor returned.

Doctor: "Well Sandye, what is your decision?"

Sandye: "Let's leave it alone. I want to go home."

The doctor was shocked.

Kent: "Sandye, what if this comes back even worse. We haven't identified the problem. I won't be able to save you at home."

Somehow, Sandye had a measure of confidence that this was the right thing to do.

Doctor: "Ok Sandye, but if you need me to perform surgery any time day or night, I will come."

While packing up preparing to be discharged, I was very nervous about what was going to happen next. A strong wind and heavy rain shook the windows. The TV beeped, alerting of a tornado warning. The diamond shaped symbol on the TV startled me. The bottom point was near the map of the area where the hospital was located. The upper point seemed to be very close to where our house was located.

Kent: "Sandye. I am not sure we should leave."

Sandye: "God has me. I want to go home."

She had a tremendous peace about it with a calm level of confidence showing on her face. I got the car and pulled under the canopy in the pouring rain. It stormed all the way home. I got her into bed but feared that something bad was going to happen. Several days passed and she started to feel better. We had no idea at the time what happened. We could not believe that we almost authorized surgery to cut her open. I truly believe that her strong faith made the difference. A few weeks later, Sandye still had stomach pains and lost a total of sixty pounds over a year's time. Our caregiver, Renae, spotted a commercial for a class action lawsuit over a blood pressure medicine called, Benicar. All the symptoms mirrored what Sandye was experiencing and she was taking it. We immediately discontinued the drug. She felt better very quickly and gained the weight back. She was far too weak to get involved in the class action suit at that time, plus we are not the ones who would file lawsuits. This was not the first malpractice lawsuit that we passed on.

Our giving ministry started to open new doors. People started bringing furniture which filled our garage. Many people were blessed, and our joy increased.

Good customers and work friends continuously supported me everywhere. Allyson Bently from Miami Dade School Doistrict, Chef T. from

Shelby County in Memphis, and Ula Kalinowski with Nardones pizza have all lifted me up with prayers, laughter and tears. I expect we will be close for eternity. Brokers, manufacture representatives and others from the southeast have loved us through the journey. There are too many to number. They respected our challenges, lifted us up, and put Sandye's needs over my work, which allowed me to return home early. I will be forever grateful.

Christmas came with many blessings. Sandye went to church wearing a bright red Christmas shirt. It had been several years since she was able to attend a Christmas service. When we came home, our small group joined us with an additional ten to fifteen people. Her friend Karen came with her two sons, Eli and Johnathan. We celebrated communion together. This was the first time her boys did that. Sandye looked thirty years younger, sitting upright and glowing with joy. Karen sang a song that she wrote called, "It Must Be Jesus." Sandye cried with sheer joy. You could cut the air with a knife and feel something special was happening right before our eyes.

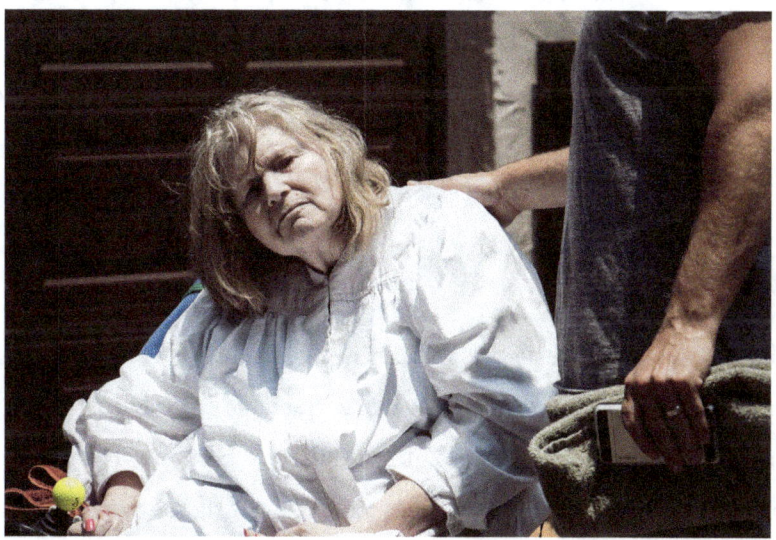

Sandye's baptism June 2016. Just before miracle.

Sandye Christmas 2016. Just after miracle.

On New Year's Eve, Brandy and Renae were sitting on the couch when I arrived home from a sales call with Gwinnett County. I went into the bedroom where Sandye was sleeping. Her eyes were closed, and her face was beet red. She appeared puzzled or in a deep dream. I called the ladies in and asked if she was like this before.

Brandy: "Absolutely not."

I had the feeling that this was something like the hospital experience after the miracle. Again, she started to awake with tears running down her face. Renae and Brandy realized that Sandye wanted to be alone, and they left. I went out to get a pad and pencil and returned waiting for Sandye to share. A few hours later she began to talk. It was very emotional.

Kent: "Did you have the same experience as before?"

Sandye: "Laymen's terms cannot describe what I experienced. Do you remember Jamie?"

Kent: "Our old neighbor's daughter?"

Sandye: "Yes."

In 2001, Terry and Connie's daughter died in a car accident near their home at the age of twenty-one.

Kent: "Did you see her?"

Sandye: "Yes. She is beautiful and in a great place (huge smile). She was completely surrounded by rainbows."

Kent: "What was it like?"

Sandye: (after a few minutes) "Layman's terms cannot describe what I experienced. The closest thing that I can compare it to is imagining myself as a four-year-old child holding my best friend's hand, skipping and laughing all the time with no worries and childlike endless joy."

We both smiled with inexpressible contentment. I wrote it down and didn't say a word, absorbing the thought and the moment. We sat in silence for many hours, enjoying God's goodness. That experience was especially draining on Sandye.

Margie and Brenda could not come to see Sandye soon enough, but Sandye needed more time to recoup. When they came, both were amazed by the transformation.

Margie: 'There's my friend. My friend is back." (huge smile)

The two glowed together.

Dr. Stuart recommended a lady, who read the featured article in the MS magazine, to call me. She read about our handicapped van ministry and knew of someone who desperately needed one. We were in the position to make that happen. Larry and Polly, who headed our small group, had planned to go with us to meet the lady at the man's house. It was a three-hour drive one way.

Sandye: "I don't think I can make it. I really wish I could."

I could see her disappointment as storm clouds roared.

Kent: "I really don't want to go without you."

A huge lightning bolt came down over the house with a huge boom. We cringed and were stunned.

Sandye: (after a moment) "No, I am good. You go ahead and go. God has me."

I walked out shaking my head in the pouring rain. I followed Larry and Polly for three hours and it never stopped raining. The visibility was near zero. As soon as we arrived at the man's house, the rain stopped abruptly. An elderly man was sitting in a wheelchair with no legs. As I got out of the van, the man started shaking both fists with joy.

Lady: "Kent, Larry and Polly, this is Larry Walker."

Kent: "Larry, it is very nice to meet you."

Larry: "Thank you, thank you, thank you ..."

Kent: "What have you been driving up until now?"

Larry: "I take my grandson, 'Baby Boy Six Van Giveaway,' to appointments in the van in the back of the house."

Kent: "Is that van accessible?"

Larry: "No."

Kent: "Would you show me the van and how you accomplish that task?"

Larry: "I even change the oil on the van."

Kent: "How in the world do you do that?"

Larry: "I drop down to the ground, lay on my back, pull

myself under the van and change the oil. Then I pull myself back out to the wheelchair."

It blew our minds that he could do that. The van was an older version.

Kent: "Can you tell me how you get in the van with your grandchild?"

Larry: "I place Baby Boy in my lap and wheel around to the back passenger door. I open the door and lift Baby Boy onto the floor in front of the back seat. Then, I lift myself onto the floor next to him. I lift Baby Boy into the seat and buckle him in. Leaning down, I grab the wheelchair, break it down and pull it over my body into the van. I then lean over to pull the passenger door shut. Then, I crawl to the driver's seat, which has hand controls. From there I can drive."

This new van would allow him to hit a remote button for the side door to open and the ramp lowered. Larry wheeled directly in and transferred himself to the driver's seat. Then, he drove around the block.

Lady: "See I told you he needed this."

When Larry wheeled down the ramp afterwards, he never stopped smiling. We asked if we could meet Baby Boy and went inside the house to transfer the title. In the living room was a cute little boy with big eyes. His cerebral palsy made him look younger than his eight years. Polly put him in her lap and joy filled the room. That one moment made every van gift we have ever donated all worth it. Larry was caring for this boy by himself. During our conversation, Larry shared that the state was trying to take Baby Boy away and the trials he endured to keep him. His story and love humbled me.

Our visit lasted an hour. After our final goodbyes, we started to drive away. Once again, the clouds opened, and the rain came down for the entire trip. I ran into the house to greet Sandye and share the pictures. The look on her face was priceless and gave her confirmation.

Larry and Baby Boy

Sandye: "Well done, Jesus."

Work kept me travelling, but I knew that I had to share this miracle with everyone. I felt like I was on a high, sharing the good news of God's miracle that I just witnessed. In a Florida conference in the middle of the event, a huge customer named, Craig Keppen, approached me. In Florida, Craig was a sought-after client. Due to past differences, the approach was not friendly. He desired to take away as much business from me. I heard that he just lost his mother. I felt the power to tell Sandye's story. This was not the usual place for that, but I felt God led. As I shared her story, we locked eyes. I could tell that he would not let himself get emotional. Based on Sandye's experience, I knew exactly where his mother was. She was in a great place. Other people tried to address him, but he was focused on my words and pushed them away. Out of character I began to speak.

Kent: "God loves you; I love you, and your mother is in a great place that Sandye has visited."

Craig was fighting back tears, stunned and we parted ways. Later that night after dinner, I was walking down the streets of Orlando. As God would have it, there was Craig coming from the other direction with an entourage of people. He told them to wait a minute and rushed towards me.

Craig: "Kent!"

It startled me.

Craig: "I just wanted to tell you that I love you too."

It blew me away. Our relationship made a complete turnaround. Our differences were healed as Craig understood my background in more detail.

At another conference in Georgia, I met up with a man named Tom, who is a vice president of a prominent company. I knew him from the past. I shared Sandye's story with him. He was very upset afterwards.

> Tom: "I threw money in the priest's face, telling them that the church was a lie. Now I have to rethink the whole thing."

> Kent: "I'm just telling you the story as I have witnessed it."

In both cases the story changed these men. One became a friend and the other returned to the church. I shared with Wayne after the Tuesday Bible study about these and other encounters happening continuously as to how lives were being changed.

> Kent: "Wayne, this is weighing heavy on me. I am sharing this story throughout the southeast to anyone who will listen. Our men's group is on a spiritual high and has doubled in size. Our story is so heavy. How do we share it with them?"

> Wayne: "Kent, this is the Holy Spirit working. We will feed it a little bit at a time and watch them grow in the Lord."

My boss now at Foster Farms, Scott Worthington, was very supportive. He listened with his wife Lita to Sandye's story and got choked up. They were willing to do anything to help us at this time. All my mentors were keeping me humble and on level ground. All the while, my sales with Foster Farms were growing exponentially. I felt like I wasn't even working while the sales results were greater than ever before. God has been taking care of me. The following Valentine's Day, I got the flu. Sandye ended up with pneumonia and went back to the hospital at Piedmont for another week. She weathered it well. As she got better, her fun side started to reappear and we laughed together. I stayed with her during those hospital stays, sleeping on a mattress on the floor. Her disability kept her from hitting the hospital button with her hands. After one bad experience with that, I would not leave her. She had been in the hospital three times in five months. Yet, with each visit she bounced back very quickly. Prior to her miracle it would have taken months. She only remembered things after her miracle and not two years before, except for her baptism day.

The president of the School Food Service and Nutrition for the state of Alabama named Dr. Bridlea Griffin, heard of Sandye's story and asked me to speak at their annual conference in Alabama. Approximately seven-hundred and fifty people from the state schools were there. It was the first week in March.

Kent: "Dr. Griffin, this story may be a conflict between church and state. Are you sure that you want me to tell it, because I am going to talk about God?"

Dr. Griffin: "We can have anyone we want to come and speak. I want you to come and tell this story."

Was I nervous! Sandye was not able to go with me, so I taped her voice. She had a froggy voice thanking them for hearing her story. On the drive to Birmingham that Friday, I stopped at a rest stop. I got on a conference call with my Friday men's group. I had trepidation about speaking God's will and asked for prayer. The men prayed for fifteen minutes, and it calmed me down. I was now in a good frame of mind. The meeting began with the color guard, the national Anthem, and formal attire. It was a well-organized state-run event. As the keynote speaker, I started the meeting. I started with the van ministry, showing pictures of recipients. You could feel the warmth in the room. Then I shared our history, showing older pictures of Sandye and I. During the account of Sandye's miracle, silence filled the room. As I got choked up, others in the room followed with tissues. I tried to play Sandye's tape, but the audio was not working. They could see her lips move but I had to speak on her behalf. I knew many of the people there from sales in the past, but this was a personal testimony.

When I stopped, it felt like I had been on a roller coaster. I put my head down and said, "Thank you Jesus." The whole room stood with a thunderous applause that blew my mind. Dr. Griffin stepped forward.

Dr. Griffin: "People in food service, especially in Alabama, are very giving and like to help others. We noticed your van ministry and want to pass the hat for a collection to help you."

Kent: "Thank you so much for the offer. I am a manufacture rep. I am not supposed to take money from customers."

Dr. Griffin: "You can't tell us what to do. We can give you money if we desire."

The money was collected. With the five-hundred dollars they paid me to speak, three-thousand dollars was raised. The people gave beyond their means, humbly and joyfully.

Kent: "I assure you that this money will help someone in dire need of a handicapped van."

During a meeting break the people flooded to the front to share how Sandye's story helped them. One lady said that her brother had recently lost a leg in a farm accident and asked for prayer. Later, I wished that I would have prayed at that moment. Another person told me that one of her colleagues was grieving over the recent loss of her husband. They had helplessly tried to comfort her over the past few months without success. The lady said that when I shared about Sandye seeing her mother in such a beautiful peaceful place, her manager expressed relief. Sandye's account was the confirmation the manager needed and could now move forward. I was feeling an overwhelming responsibility about what the Lord was doing in my life.

After that conference in Alabama, I decided to match the $3000 and purchase a van to bring it back the for the next years conference. Fast forwarding one year, I prayed that God would bring someone forward that really needed that van. About a month before the conference, I received a call from one of the directors in Homewood, Alabama telling me they had someone in need. One of the cafeteria employees at Homewood High School was currently lifting her granddaughter, who had cerebral palsy, up into a car everyday to take her to school. It was difficult for her to accomplish this task without getting hurt. This was a perfect opportunity. The day before the conference, two men from my "Old Man's Bible Study" drove over to Homewood in the van. The lady was told to dress up that day for they were going to someone's place for prayer at lunch. As they walked around the corner, the whole cafeteria's staff, the Foodservice director and the State's directors in authority were there to surprise her. I walked up a bit nervous. She was looking stunned and totally shocked. She thought she was going to someones house to pray.

> Kent: "Hello, I am Kent. We heard that you needed a van for
> your granddaughter and to make your life a little bit easier.
> This van behind me is now yours. "

The whole staff exploded in cheers and tears were flowing. I was speechless which says a lot. She threw her arms around and firmly hugged me. It quieted down. After taking a second to process the moment she spoke.

> Grandmother: "Just when I thought nobody cared, Jesus is
> all up in this place."

Her granddaughter was cheering wildly as we took pictures with all the people that made this happen. It was amazing to see what God was doing. We videoed the event to show it to all the people at the conference dinner the next night.

Dr. Brindlea Griffen, Mrs. Kat and family, Kent, Erin (Foodservice Diector), and Dr. Ashley Powell 7th Van Giveaway

While waiting for the next night to come, my two friends who came with me, Rob and Kip, pondered what we were experiencing. We were going to the grand premiere of the first showing of the movie "I can only Imagine." The Irwin Brothers who made the movie are originally from Alabama. Some of the school directors had gone to the same church with them. This was only fitting for I have loved that song and their story for years. God's timing is perfect! When Saturday night came and we attended the banquet in Birmingham, Alabama, I called the grandmother and her manager up to the stage. They were in beautiful dresses, and I shared the story. As the video concluded, the people in the room jumped to their feet and erupted with cheer and praise. There was not a dry eye in the ballroom. I also shared the miracle progress that Sandye had made since I last spoke about her one year prior. Then I finished and had to leave immediately to get back to

Sandye that night. The next speaker came on.

> Speaker: "I cannot follow that emotion. Let's give Kent a
> moment to leave the room."

As my friends and I gathered our things and walked all the way across the large ballroom passing six-hundred people, you could not hear a word spoken. It was as if they were honoring the moment. It felt reverent. You could feel something special in the air that moved everyone present. As I was driving home, I started shaking with excitement, calling my friends and telling them the great news of what I just experienced. How could giving and sharing Gods story feel like no other feeling I had ever had, WOW! I developed a close relationship with the School Food Service directors and managers in Alabama that would last forever. These people were now family and walking out our story with us. This was a magical night. I ended up speaking three years in a row at that conference, which was a first for testimonies at the state-run School Foodservice meetings.

Wendall Tarkington, who had been part of our faith walk for the past fifteen years, was very interested in sharing our story with his Methodist church that we used to attend. Because Sandye had been in and out of the hospital so many times recently, he was concerned that she would not survive to tell her story. The pastor at the Methodist church that we had attended named, Mathew Mitchell, agreed to have me share the story as soon as possible to the church. I drove down with a friend from one of my men's groups. My emotions were heightened due to the last six months.

> Kent: "I love her so much. I just want to honor God in these
> moments."

Willis: (man in car) "Kent, you are loving her like Jesus loves all of us."

Being previous members, many great memories hit me as I entered the church. I first spoke to a small group with Wendall and Mathew. About thirty people were present and I shared the whole story. Like the other times, you could feel the Holy Spirit in the room. Pastor Mathew was very excited to share this message with the whole church. After that meeting a lady came to me with a picture of Jesus.

Lady: "Please ask your wife if this is what He looked like."

Later, I asked Sandye about Jesus' appearance. She maintained that she never saw His face but rested on His lap. I went on the stage with pastor Mathew. Approximately, four-hundred people were there, including men from my Tuesday Bible study. Again, this group was moved to tears. I knew that God had control. Pastor Mathew captured the heavy rain mentioned throughout our story. Prior to the service, he placed hundreds of bottles of water on the steps in front of the stage.

Pastor Mathew: "As the powerful rush of water was shared in Kent and Sandye's story, let the water flow into you. Come down to the stage and pray. Take the symbolic water with you."

As we finished, many came forward. A pastor from my men's group came to me.

Pastor: "In fifty years, I never saw a Methodist congregation held silent for forty-five minutes until now."

Another man shared that his wife recently passed away and this story gave him a greatly needed peace. Everyone knew that God was doing powerful things. I was being obedient.

Sandye was about to turn sixty. I never thought this day would come a year ago. She was still very fragile and our groups were in constant prayer for her strength. Her friend, Brenda, had planned to make the trip up for Sandye's birthday as usual but Sandye was too weak. Side effects from the infusion would have been too much for the visit. We asked Brenda not to come. Two days before her birthday, she had an infusion scheduled. That Sunday, our group could see her weakened condition and prayed for her to have the strength to handle the infusion. It was a new drug on the market. The affects of pneumonia were still evident. In the infusion room, before the IV was administered, out of nowhere, Sandye perked up and started acting surprisingly energetic..

Sandye: "I feel really good."

Kent: "Ok."

Knowing what happened a year before, I didn't see this coming.

Sandye: "I want to do something big for my birthday"

Kent: "Ok. What do you want to do?"

Sandye: "I want to go skydiving."

Flashbacks came into my mind of times when she was scared, especially of heights. She was afraid of falling three feet. A Ferris wheel ride made her dig her nails into my arms. Now she desired to go to fourteen-thousand feet. It was amazing that she had a new burst of energy before she had even received the infusion. Our prayers were for her to have enough strength to handle the medicine. Unbelievably, now she wants to do this. If she was going to dream, I was going to dream with her.

I picked up the phone and immediately called skydiving companies in the area. We located one about two-hour drive away that would accommodate us. We planned to go on her birthday on Friday, two days later. I called Brenda after these remarkable events.

> Kent: "I can't explain this turn around, Brenda. I would love for you to come. I will even fly you up. I know it's a moment's notice."

> Brenda: "No. If she is able to do this, go ahead and go. I have already been skydiving and we don't know what is going to happen, anyway."

We had cancelled many events in the past due to health issues.

> Brenda: "Know that I will never change my mind again in the future, knowing that God has His own plans."

The day arrived. I told Sandye that I would jump with her.

Sandye: "No. You have already done it. This is a girl's event.
I want Brandy to jump with me."

Brandy's eyes opened wide as if to say, "Who me...jump out of a plane."
After seeing all that Sandye had been through the past year, Brandy agreed.
I helped Brandy get a job in the food industry and knew that she would be
able to go on such short notice. Steve, insisted on going with us. I called
Russ and Leslie and asked if they wanted to join us. They could not make
that happen in such short notice. The reservation was made for a specific
time so that she would not have to wait, due to the limitations of her body.

On the trip we picked up Steve, who was in a bad mood. Sandye and I
were not having that and were celebrating the entire way.

Sandye: "It's birthday, YAYYYY!!!"

At first, Steve did not want to hear that but we were going to wear him
down. On arrival, we had to sign numerous forms as if to sign our life away.

Brandy: "Are you sure we have to go through this?"

Kent: "Just sign."

We began to wait as they were well behind. We watched other skydivers
land near us. I could see Sandye's body start to fail from fatigue as it does
later in the afternoon. A young man sat beside me. I thought he was there
to view the event. I shared with him how important this day was and how

important it was for the person who jumped with her to also protect her. He worked for the company. He introduced himself as Kyle.

Kyle: "Let me see what I can do."

He left and went inside the building. Then he called us to get ready. I had shared that Sandye could not move her arms or legs and how important it was for her to be protected during landing.

Kyle: "Sir. I moved the schedule around. I am going to jump with her."

He was a strong young man, and I knew this would be good for Sandye. I stood her up and held her while they slipped a harness over her body. Just before it was time to go, a lady walked up, who was going to video their jump.

Lady: "I assume you're Sandye by your cake hat. It must be your special day to jump. I am going to film your jump. My name is Leslie."

Sandye and I stared at each other in shock. It was as if our best friend Leslie,and her son Kyle were there to make the jump with her even though they were not able to physically come. That blew Russ' mind as we shared later. After a short video, we went out to the tarmac to help load Sandye onto the plane. Usually, spectators were not allowed but I needed to provide physical support. The plane pulled up. All the crew, jumpers and helpers climbed the stairs into the open area of the plane. I gave Steve my phone to video while I moved Sandye's chair in front of the opening. Kyle, two other men and I lifted her up onto the floor of the plane. Then the others lifted her into a seat on the plane. Kyle put his arm around her to keep her from falling. We backed up and watched the plane pull away. When the noise lessened I shared my thoughts with Steve.

Kent: "Come back to me safe my love." (tears running down my cheeks)

Steve: "Oh my God, I have never felt anything like this." (Excited)

It was much harder for me to watch then if I had gone with her, because I was not there to protect her. After watching the video, I was able to share what occurred next. I was concerned for the height being too much for her, but Sandye was in a different place. Leslie, the photographer, went over to Sandye on the plane.

Leslie: "Sandye. We are at four-thousand feet so far. How do you feel?"

Sandye: "Great. Are you going to give me shiny goggles to wear?"

Leslie: "Oh yeah."

You could see Brandy behind her with a nervous smile of anticipation. At fourteen-thousand feet, Leslie stepped out of the plane on the wing, still clinging to a handle. She videoed Kyle lifting Sandye up and attaching clips that connected the two of them. He carried her to the door opening. Most people are told to arch their back, but Sandye was not able to do that. Kyle knew this would cause a problem that might flip them backwards. When they leaped out, they immediately went into the backflip. Thank God that Kyle knew what he was doing. Now they were falling a hundred-eighty miles per hour, while Leslie captured everything on tape. Sandye slumped down but with a huge smile on her face. No clouds were in the sky which was a beautiful blue. On the horizon appeared a silver lining. Kyle and Leslie used hand movements as signals during the fall. Kyle covered his eyes with his hands as a signal to Leslie, if Sandye looked okay. Leslie gave him a thumbs up. During the fall, Sandye asked Kyle to pull her right hand up like everyone else. After struggling through the wind, he was able to raise her hand. A huge smile came on her face.

Soon after, Kyle gave the sign to pull his chute. Inadvertently, he let go of Sandye's arm to signal and wondered if he had hurt her. Sandye continued to smile. As Kyle pulled the ripcord for the chute, Leslie kept falling to video their landing. We positioned ourself in the field with her wheelchair, which the company permitted. We watched people land over the four-hundred-yard field. All the others were landing before Sandye, although she jumped first. Kyle took her for a ride. As Steve and I watched, we screamed at all the others landing. It was out of this world. We could see Brandy coming in close to us at a high rate of speed. She picked her feet up as instructed, while her partner absorbed the fall, bouncing several times. Brandy jumped with joy and looked hurt exercising her shoulder but didn't care.

Now it was Sandye's turn. We were screaming at her. "Come on Home." They could have landed anywhere but came directly towards us. Kyle kicked her feet out about fifteen feet from us, leaned back, and took all the weight on the fall. He sacrificed himself for her safety. Leslie ran up while videoing.

Sandye after landing (wheelchair in back)

Sandye taking the plunge

Sandye soaring

Leslie: "Sandye. What do you think?"

Sandye: "It was too fast. I am sorry that my body didn't cooperate."

Leslie: "It doesn't matter. You went skydiving."

Sandye: "YAYYY."

Kyle had a big smile on his face that he would never forget. Brandy ran over to Sandye and hugged her.

Brandy: "You did it. You did it."

I stepped in and gave Sandye a big kiss.

Kent: "I knew you would come back to me."

We pulled the wheelchair over and placed her in it. The drive home seemed like we were floating, due to all the excitement. Steve led the cheers.

Steve: "YAYYY!"

Sandye: "I felt free at last."

The news spread through our entire group. We planned to view the video on Sunday when the group was coming over. Steve came ten minutes before everyone.

Steve: "YAYYYYYY!"

We both laughed and rejoiced. The mood was festive as everyone brought food. Steve would scream our signature "yay" cheer several times as people had no idea what he was doing. Then he grinned at me. About forty people came. I went in to talk to Sandye who was tired from the week. Often, she stayed in bed and did not attend.

Sandye: "I have to get up and see them today."

I helped her get dressed and said that I would return after a few minutes. In the living room, two large groups gathered and were eating. It sounded like a large party. I went back for Sandye and brought her in. Once again

Steve screamed.

Steve: "YAYYYYYYYYYY!!!!!!!!"

A massive roar of applause exploded in the room when Sandye entered. They realized what Steve was doing. It settled down and Sandye was sitting at a table talking. I stood in the middle of the room with Rene, an elder from the church.

Rene: "Listen to that Kent. Can you hear it? The excitement in this house is so powerful."

We stopped for a moment and took it all in. It was a moment in time that we would remember forever. After eating, we watched the video of Sandye skydiving with families of all ages. Some cheered. Some ducked their heads in fear when she jumped from the plane. Everyone was amazed what God had done. You could feel it. I learned to have joy through all the journeys in life, no matter the difficulty or the obstacles. Sandye always made it a point to never look back, only forward. Joy is a choice, and we choose it. The love shown through all these people and the other groups is what got us through. It will be great to tell the rest of this story. You haven't seen anything yet. Our test is our testimony for God's glory!

Chip, chip, chip. The master's work begins to glow. Those who look upon it see love, joy and peace. There is still more to do, but the imperfections are hardly noticeable. The artist steps back and admires all that has been accomplished.

Jeremiah 18:6 (NIV)

"As the clay is in the potters hand, so are you in my hand."

Epilogue

L ooking back thirty years, I marvel how far we have come. I cannot believe that guy who was driving across the country in a broken-down van is the same person. How did we make it through all these trials and continue to thrive? I can see how, as we drew closer to God, He removed many of our faults. We are a work in progress with a long way to go. As we grow in the Lord our heart for giving becomes one our biggest blessings. Giving to others took the focus off impossible situations and allowed for us to celebrate the joys of life. Giving, worshipping and bonding with like-minded positive people helped us look forward to the next joyful journey. Finding a support system of friends and family is crucial to keep our heads above water. We are not meant to endure this journey alone.

I cannot describe the depth of my love for Sandye and what she has meant to me. She stayed with me all during my brokenness which gave me the strength to take care of her year after year. As the struggle became harder, we worked at growing together through every challenge. Sandye never gave up and always fought for her faith. Though her body failed externally, her spiritual relationship grew stronger and stronger. She never blamed God for her ruthless and progressive disease. She maintained that "God didn't give her the disease but was there for her when she got it," and "MS will never define her."

Why did God pick us? I do not feel worthy. Then I realized all the people He chose over the years were also flawed. The fact is, He knows everyone's heart and guides us if we let Him. I know, by Sandye's brief journey spending time in Jesus' lap, the incredible place that is waiting for us called Heaven. So, if you have lost someone dear, struggle to care for a family member, watch someone battle addictions, or any other daily struggle, I am here to tell you that God desires to help you. Trust Him and He will lead you through victoriously. If we can do it and have complete joy, so can you. Saying thank you to Jesus is not enough, but it will have to do for now.

My life has been changed beyond human words. The absence of love from my father and my reckless lifestyle no longer is a thought or an option. Although, we are still a work in progress if we will just let God in and let Him work in us. I still have a long way to go. This relationship with God and Sandye brings true Joy through the Journey. The love of my wife and God has filled me with unending Joy that goes way beyond anything that I could have imagined. This is not the end of our story. It just gets better and better. You're not going to believe what happens next. Stay tuned.

Nothing is impossible as long as you stay thirsty and believe.

Sandye and Kent 2019